WHAT DID JESUS SAY ABOUT AUTHORITY?

RALPH GOOD

What Did Jesus Say About Authority?

Table of Contents

FORWARD

Searching the Scriptures for answers about authority, I discovered something over 25 years ago no nobody ever taught in the church. The Greek word exousia[G1849], most often translated as *authority*, also translates as *power*. This same Greek word defines in many verses the power and authority of God's kingdom and Satan's kingdom.

I have been in church for over 35 years and never heard any authorities in the church even attempt to distinguish between the power and authority ascribed by Scripture with the same Greek word, *exousia*[G1849], to both kingdoms. I am shocked and dismayed, as I now realize that as a young believer with little knowledge of the Bible, I was forced, by misuse of Scripture, to submit to authorities exercising principles of authority Scripture ascribes to Satan's kingdom of darkness. Yet, these authorities claimed to be "God's delegated authority."They nearly destroyed my life as I refused to submit to them. I am not saying they had evil intent. I believe Satan blinded them because of their lack of knowledge as to what Jesus said about authority.

Outraged, I sought God's guidance. After decades of prayer and study, His answer came: bring the issue before the church.

Chapter 1

Questions About Submitting to Authority

Romans 13:1–2 (NKJV)
Let every soul be subject to the governing authorities. For there is no authority except from God, and the authorities that exist are appointed by God. Therefore whoever resists the authority resists the ordinance of God, and those who resist will bring judgment on themselves.

Titus 3:1 (NKJV)
Remind them to be subject to rulers and authorities, to obey, to be ready for every good work.

Hebrews 13:17 (NKJV)
Obey those who rule over you, and be submissive, for they watch out for your souls, as those who must give account. Let them do so with joy and not with grief, for that would be unprofitable for you.

What Did Jesus Say About Authority?

1 Peter 2:13 (NKJV)
> Therefore submit yourselves to every ordinance of man for the Lord's sake, whether to the king as supreme, or to governors, as to those who are sent by him for the punishment of evildoers and *for the* praise of those who do good.

Question 1

If we believe these passages of Scripture to be true, then why do we teach our children in our Sunday schools to do the opposite? We teach our children to model their lives after the great heroes of the Christian faith who openly defied the authorities God placed in their lives and faced judgment.

The following are heroes in the Bible who we teach our children to follow.

Stephen–A devout and godly man, Stephen was a deacon in the church and totally committed to the cause of Christ. He openly confronted the council, including the High Priest, for being stiff-necked, resisting the Holy Spirit, killing the prophets, and mistreating God's Anointed One, the Christ, whom they killed. These authorities judged Stephen for confronting their misuse of God's authority, dragged him out of town, and stoned him to death. We teach our children that Stephen is a hero! (Acts 7.)

Shadrach, Meshach, and Abed-Nego –These three

godly men wholeheartedly served God and the king, but they refused to submit to the king's decree and bow to his golden idol, *a violation of the first commandment*. This infuriated the king, who passed judgment on them for their disobedience to his commands. So outraged, he threw them into the fiery furnace. We proclaim Shadrach, Meshach, and Abed-Nego as heroes to our children in our Sunday schools! (Dan. 3.)

Daniel –For openly resisting the king's decree and facing judgment for his disobedience in the lion's den, we proclaim Daniel a hero. We even teach our children that he is someone to emulate! (Dan. 6.)

David –As a lad, with five stones and a slingshot, David stood up to a giant while the whole army of God's people trembled in fear. Later, David ran for his life from God's anointed who was trying to kill him. This conflict did not happen because David did something wrong or had a problem with authority—but because the authority God put in his life, Saul, had a problem with God. King Saul made a premeditated decision to use 3,000 Special Forces in an attempt to kill God's anointed, the forefather of the promised Messiah. King Saul killed85 priests of God, and their wives and children, for helping David, the man after God's own heart, escape the king's malicious judgment! (1 Sam. 17–24.)

Peter –He defied the council's orders and continued to proclaim the name of the Lord, claiming with the other apostles, "We ought to obey God rather than men!" (Acts 5:29 NKJV) and "We must obey God rather than any human authority" (NLT).

Then there are Esther, Moses, Gideon, Paul, John the Baptist, and Jesus Christ Himself, usually in conflict with the religious authorities God established. Jesus even called some of those who considered themselves to be "authorities" sons of their father, the devil!(John 8:44.)

All of these people—and many more—faced judgment for resisting authorities God established.

We teach our children to emulate these heroes of the Bible who faced judgment, even death, because they did what Jesus Christ said is the most important thing to do in the Holy Bible: *honor the first commandment*. God, and His Word, must be honored—above all, before all, and at all times—regardless of the cost—including that of their own lives!

Luke 12:4–5 (NKJV)
> And I say to you, My friends, do not be afraid of those who kill the body, and after that have no more that they can do. But I will show you whom you should fear: Fear Him who, after He has killed, has power to cast into hell; yes, I say to you, fear Him!

My brethren, who claim to be God's delegated authority in the church, I ask you. At what point in the life of believers—from when we paint murals of these scenes in our nurseries and proclaim them to be the gospel truth—are believers required to submit to the implied infallibility of authorities in the local church, and their vision, before their personal relationship with Jesus Christ, which is *a violation of the first commandment*?

Causing anyone to violate the first commandment separates them from God, the source of life, and leads to their spiritual death. Such "works of ministry" violate and reject the responsibilities of the Great Commission appointed to the church by Jesus Christ!

Question 2

In Revelation 13, Scripture identifies an individual who will rise with great authority and rule every tribe, tongue, and nation. He will issue laws forbidding anyone to buy and sell unless you submit to taking his number, 666.

This causes a serious dilemma.

Are we, as Christians, required by God to submit to the authority Scripture identifies as being of Satan, the Beast, the kingdom of darkness, and the rulers of this world? Scripture verses detailing this power and authority are provided in Chapters 4 and 7.

Would we be guilty of resisting God, and the authorities God established, if we resist the authority Scripture attributes to Satan, the god of this world, the Beast, the kingdom of darkness, and the rulers of this world?

Of course *NOT*! The Bible says in Ephesians 6:12 that our battle is against the rulers, the authorities, and the powers of this world!

However, refusing to submit to them will bring the judgment of death from the one Scripture says has been given great authority over every tribe, tongue, and nation!

Did the power and authority Scripture attributes to Satan, the Beast, the kingdom of darkness, and the rulers of this world originate from God, given that the Bible teaches us"our battle is against them"?

Yes, the authority of Satan originated from God. However, God gave this authority to Adam at creation. Satan, in his craftiness, stole it from Adam and misused it to fulfill his own vision! Thus, Satan became the ruler of this world instead of man. Satan, by his deception, deceived Adam into violating God's command and separated humanity from God. Thus, we fell under the influence of the power and authority of Satan and his kingdom of darkness, dooming us to eternal damnation!

But God so loved the world that He sent His only Son Jesus Christ. He was the only human not under the power and authority of Satan because of the virgin birth. He refused to violate the first commandment! He withstood Satan's temptations and made a public spectacle of him on the cross. He delivered us from the power and authority of Satan and his kingdom of darkness. With His blood, He removed the separation between God and Man, established the New Covenant, and restored our God-given rights to the authority that Adam lost to Satan. This same Jesus gave us "Our God Given Rights to the Fullness of Our Salvation"[1] and all the spiritual blessings of the redeemed—a blessed inheritance with Christ in Heaven.

Luke 10:18–20 (NKJV)
> And He said to them, "I saw Satan fall like lightning from heaven. Behold, I give you the authority to trample on serpents and scorpions, and over all the power of the enemy, and nothing shall by any means hurt you. Nevertheless do not rejoice in this, that the spirits are subject to you, but rather rejoice because your names are written in heaven."

Colossians 1:13–14 (NKJV)
> He has delivered us from the power of darkness and conveyed *us* into the kingdom of the Son of His love, in whom we have redemption through His blood, the forgiveness of sins.

Revelations 12:10–11 (NKJV)
> Then I heard a loud voice saying in heaven,

---

[1]To learn more, visit www.ourgodgivenrights.com and down load a free PDF copy or buy a print edition of my previous book *OUR GOD-GIVEN RIGHTS: To the Fullness of Our Salvation and the Vast Demonic Conspiracy.*

"Now salvation, and strength, and the kingdom of our God, and the power of His Christ have come, for the accuser of our brethren, who accused them before our God day and night, has been cast down. And they overcame him by the blood of the Lamb and by the word of their testimony, and they did not love their lives to the death."

James 4:7 (NKJV)

Therefore submit to God. Resist the devil and he will flee from you.

1 Peter 5:8–9 (NKJV)

Be sober; be vigilant; because your adversary the devil walks about like a roaring lion, seeking whom he may devour. Resist him, steadfast in the faith, knowing that the same sufferings are experienced by your brotherhood in the world.

Question 3

In Matthew 20:25, Mark 10:42, and Luke 22:25, Jesus Christ used four Greek words—*katakurieuo*, *katexousiazo*, *kurieuo*, and *exousiazo*—to define those authorities of this world that He taught does not belong among His people. (A detailed study appears in Chapter 4.) Below, these four words are defined using *Thayer's Greek Dictionary*.[2]

---

[2]Joseph Henry Thayer, *Thayer's Greek Dictionary* (Cedar Rapids, IA: Parsons Technology, Inc.).

What Did Jesus Say About Authority?

katakurieuo
Pronunciation: *kat-ak-oo-ree-yoo'-o*
1. to bring under one's power, to subject one's self, to subdue, master
2. to hold in subjection, to be master of, exercise lordship over

katexousiazo
Pronunciation: *kat-ex-oo-see-ad'-zo*
1. to exercise authority, wield power

kurieuo
Pronunciation: *koo-ree-you'-o*
1. to be lord of, to rule, have dominion over
2. of things and forces
2a) to exercise influence upon, to have power over

exousiazo
Pronunciation: *ex-oo-see-ad'-zo*
1. to have power or authority, use power
1a. to be master of any one, exercise authority over one
1b. to be master of the body
1b1.to have full and entire authority over the body
1b2. to hold the body subject to one's will
1c.to be brought under the power of anyone

Do we have a biblical obligation to entrust and submit our lives to authorities in the local church practicing these worldly principles of authority, when Jesus Christ clearly told us, "It shall not be so among you?"

Would we be guilty of resisting God, and authorities God established, if we obey the teachings of Jesus Christ by, *honoring the first commandment?* And thereby, refuse to submit to authorities in the local church to do "works of ministry" when they engage these worldly principles of authority.

Is their judgment equal to God's judgment if we do not submit; or, is this judgment from men using fear of judgment as a dominating, controlling mechanism to enslave people to fulfill their own vision?

Submitting to or allowing ourselves to be subdued, overcome, and/or dominated by authorities practicing these worldly principles brings us again under bondage to principles of authority of this world, whose ruler is Satan. If we give in to the "fear of judgment," they may impose upon us; we would become useless to God, separated from Him as they become first in our lives instead of God, *violating the first commandment.* Thus, we would forfeit our ability to walk in the grace given by Jesus Christ, which, in turn, would render us powerless to exercise our God-given rights to the power, authority, and freedoms Jesus restored to us on the cross.[3]Consequently, we would live in defeat!

---

[3] To learn more about *OUR GOD-GIVEN RIGHTS*, visit www.ourgodgivenrights.

So how can authorities in the church engaging in these worldly principles of authority to motivate people to do "works of ministry" legitimately claim to be "God's delegated authority" while they defy and rebel against the teachings of Jesus Christ, the head of the Church?

Those who do such a thing are unlawfully engaging in principles of authority Jesus Christ defined as being of this world. Scripture is clear: Jesus Christ has forbidden this among His people. Therefore, it is deceitful and unjust for authorities in the local church to justify passing judgment on God's people for "rebelling against," or "having a problem with," authority when believers refuse to submit to these worldly principles of authority. These believers rightly follow the teachings of Jesus Christ by refusing to submit to the principles that do not belong among His people—they instead *honor the first commandment*. As Paul affirms, "Our battle is against the rulers and authorities of this world" (Eph. 6:12).

Question 4

Protestant, Evangelical, and Pentecostal clergy do not believe in or submit to the pope's infallible authority.

All these clergies believe they have the God-given right and authority, as New Covenant believers, to seek and determine God's will for their own lives through personal prayer and study of Scripture, independent from the pope's authority.

So, is the origin of the pope's authority from God?

If it is, why do these clergy not submit to the pope?

If the origin of the pope's authority is not from God, then an authority exists, recognized by millions, whose origin has not been established by God!

So then, if the origin of the pope's authority is not from God, and therefore, we do not have to submit to his authority, then how many other authorities exist that have *not* been established by God and that we have no Biblical obligation to follow? Furthermore, how can we tell the difference between those established by God and those not established by God?

Authorities in most Christian denominations, non-denominations, inter-dominations, local churches, and many known religious cults in some way, at least in part, claim Scripture to legitimize their authority as established by God. In addition, they use Scripture to justify passing judgment on those who refuse to submit to their expression of authority.

Therefore, I ask: what makes the authority in one group more relevant and/or infallible than the authority in another group when they do not agree? Some contradict each other. Some taint their followers against authorities in other groups. Some go as far as calling the authority in another group the antichrist. These actions do not reflect the prayer of our Lord in John 17, who established authorities in the church to bring us into the unity of the faith, the fullness of His redemption, and invited all to sit together at the marriage feast of the Lamb!

When authorities insist "All authority is of God," which usually means, *my* authority is of God (*not* the pope's), and if you resist me, you will receive judgment. Such actions are a form of dominance akin to the four Greek words Jesus Christ used to define authority of this world! It certainly does not demonstrate the servant-hood Christ Jesus, the Head of the church, demonstrated with His own life for His servants to follow.

All authority is of God includes:
- The authority of Scripture, the only infallible authority for our faith.
- The authority of Jesus Christ, the Head of the church, who appointed all authorities in the church to bring believers into their God-given rights to the fullness of their salvation bestowed on them by Jesus.
- The authority of the New Covenant believer, which gives each Christian the God-given right and authority, to go to God themselves through the blood of Christ to discern God's will for their own lives. Jesus gave them this God-given right with the fullness of their salvation so they can honor

the first commandment—by keeping God first in their lives.

Denying believers, this God-given right and authority to discern God's will for their own lives—keep God first—usurps and rejects the authority of Jesus Christ, the Head of the church, who gave them this God-given right with the fullness of their salvation. Remember: Jesus Christ redeemed every believer with His own blood and gave this God-given right and authority with the fullness of their salvation because of their belief in Him as the Son of God, their Lord and Savior.

Therefore, to deny anybody these God-given rights and authority included with the fullness of their salvation, is to deny them Christ and what He did for them on the cross! Such "works of ministry" that denies believers any of their God-given rights and authority bestowed upon them with Christ's precious gift of salvation is not of God![4]

So, how can any authority that denies, oppresses, and/or even rejects the rights and authority of the New Covenant believer to seek God's will for their own lives—to *honor the first commandment*—legitimately claim to be of God? God sent His only Son to die on the cross to establish the rights and authority of the New Covenant believer!

---

[4] To learn more about *OUR GOD GIVEN-RIGHTS TO THE FULLNESS OF OUR SALVATION,* visit www.ourgodgivenrights.com.

What Did Jesus Say About Authority?

True spiritual authority will always acknowledge, honor, and respect the God-given rights, authority and freedoms of the New Covenant bestowed to them with their precious gift of salvation to *honor the first commandment.* **This is what Jesus said is the most important thing any believer can do.** True-delegated authorities will *never* lead us to *violate the first commandment.* Doing so would separate people from God, the source of all life, and lead to our spiritual death. Satan did just that to Adam and Eve in the Garden of Eden.

Question 5

Suppose all authority is of God, as Scripture says, and we must submit to all authorities in our lives or face judgment, as so often taught in church. Why then does Jesus Christ, in God's Word, repeatedly warn us to take heed, watch out for, and be aware of those who are or claim to be in God-ordained positions of authority?

Mark 13:9 (NLT)
> "When these things begin to happen, watch out!
> You will be handed over to the local councils
> and beaten in the synagogues. You will stand
> trial before governors and kings because you are
> my followers. But this will be your opportunity
> to tell them about me."

Ephesians 6:12 (NLT)
> For we are not fighting against flesh-and-blood
> enemies, but against evil rulers and authorities of

the unseen world, against mighty powers in this dark world, and against evil spirits in the heavenly places.

Matthew 7:15–16 (NKJV)
"Beware of false prophets, who come to you in sheep's clothing, but inwardly they are ravenous wolves. You will know them by their fruits. Do men gather grapes from thornbushes or figs from thistles?"

Matthew 15:8–9 (NKJV)
"These people draw near to Me with their mouth, And honor Me with their lips, But their heart is far from Me. And in vain they worship Me, Teaching as doctrines the commandments of men."

Matthew 16:6 (NKJV)
Then Jesus said to them, "Take heed and beware of the leaven of the Pharisees and the Sadducees."

Matthew 23:13 (NKJV)
"But woe to you, scribes and Pharisees, hypocrites! For you shut up the kingdom of heaven against men; for you neither go in *yourselves,* nor do you allow those who are entering to go in."

Matthew 23:15 (NKJV)
"Woe to you, scribes and Pharisees, hypocrites! For you travel land and sea to win one proselyte,

and when he is won, you make him twice as much a son of hell as yourselves."

Matthew 23:23–24 (NKJV)
"Woe to you, scribes and Pharisees, hypocrites! For you pay tithe of mint and anise and cummin, and have neglected the weightier *matters* of the law: justice and mercy and faith. These you ought to have done, without leaving the others undone. Blind guides, who strain out a gnat and swallow a camel!"

Matthew 23:25–26 (NKJV)
"Woe to you, scribes and Pharisees, hypocrites! For you cleanse the outside of the cup and dish, but inside they are full of extortion and self-indulgence. Blind Pharisee, first cleanse the inside of the cup and dish, that the outside of them may be clean also."

Matthew 23:27–28 (NKJV)
"Woe to you, scribes and Pharisees, hypocrites! For you are like whitewashed tombs which indeed appear beautiful outwardly, but inside are full of dead *men's* bones and all uncleanness. Even so you also outwardly appear righteous to men, but inside you are full of hypocrisy and lawlessness."

Matthew 24:4–5 (NKJV)
And Jesus answered and said to them: "Take heed that no one deceives you. For many will come in My name, saying, 'I am the Christ,' and

will deceive many."

Matthew 24:23–25 (NKJV)

"Then if anyone says to you, 'Look, here *is* the Christ!' or 'There!' do not believe *it*. For false christs and false prophets will rise and show great signs and wonders to deceive, if possible, even the elect. See, I have told you beforehand."

Mark 12:38–40 (NKJV)

Then He said to them in His teaching, "Beware of the scribes, who desire to go around in long robes, *love* greetings in the marketplaces, the best seats in the synagogues, and the best places at feasts, who devour widows' houses, and for a pretense make long prayers. These will receive greater condemnation."

Mark 13:21–23 (NKJV)

"Then if anyone says to you, 'Look, here *is* the Christ!' or, 'Look, *He is* there!' do not believe it. For false christs and false prophets will rise and show signs and wonders to deceive, if possible, even the elect. But take heed; see, I have told you all things beforehand.

Luke 17:22–23 (NKJV)

Then He said to the disciples, "The days will come when you will desire to see one of the days of the Son of Man, and you will not see *it*. And they will say to you, 'Look here!' or 'Look there!' Do not go after *them* or follow *them*.

What Did Jesus Say About Authority?

Luke 21:8–9 (NKJV)

And He said: "Take heed that you not be deceived. For many will come in My name, saying, 'I am *He,*' and, 'The time has drawn near.' Therefore do not go after them. But when you hear of wars and commotions, do not be terrified; for these things must come to pass first, but the end *will not come* immediately."

1 Corinthians 7:23 (NKJV)

You were bought at a price; do not become slaves of men.

Galatians 2:4–5 (NKJV)

And *this occurred* because of false brethren secretly brought in (who came in by stealth to spy out our liberty which we have in Christ Jesus, that they might bring us into bondage), to whom we did not yield submission even for an hour, that the truth of the gospel might continue with you.

Galatians 5:1 (NKJV)

Stand fast therefore in the liberty by which Christ has made us free, and do not be entangled again with a yoke of bondage.

Galatians 5:7 (NKJV)

You ran well. Who hindered you from obeying the truth?

Ephesians 4:14 (NKJV)

. . . That we should no longer be children, tossed

to and fro and carried about with every wind of doctrine, by the trickery of men, in the cunning craftiness of deceitful plotting.

Ephesians 5:6–7 (NKJV)
Let no one deceive you with empty words, for because of these things the wrath of God comes upon the sons of disobedience. Therefore do not be partakers with them.

Colossians 2:8–10 (NKJV)
Beware lest anyone cheat you through philosophy and empty deceit, according to the tradition of men, according to the basic principles of the world, and not according to Christ. For in Him dwells all the fullness of the Godhead bodily; and you are complete in Him, who is the head of all principality and power.

Colossians 2:18–19 (NKJV)
Let no one cheat you of your reward, taking delight in *false* humility and worship of angels, intruding into those things which he has not seen, vainly puffed up by his fleshly mind, and not holding fast to the Head, from whom all the body, nourished and knit together by joints and ligaments, grows with the increase *that is* from God.

1 Timothy 4:1–3 (NKJV)
Now the Spirit expressly says that in latter times some will depart from the faith, giving heed to deceiving spirits and doctrines of demons,

speaking lies in hypocrisy, having their own conscience seared with a hot iron, forbidding to marry, *and commanding* to abstain from foods which God created to be received with thanksgiving by those who believe and know the truth.

Titus 1:10–11 (NKJV)
For there are many insubordinate, both idle talkers and deceivers, especially those of the circumcision, whose mouths must be stopped, who subvert whole households, teaching things which they ought not, for the sake of dishonest gain.

Titus 1:16 (NKJV)
They profess to know God, but in works they deny Him, being abominable, disobedient, and disqualified for every good work.

2 Peter 2:1–3 (NKJV)
But there were also false prophets among the people, even as there will be false teachers among you, who will secretly bring in destructive heresies, even denying the Lord who bought them, *and* bring on themselves swift destruction. And many will follow their destructive ways, because of whom the way of truth will be blasphemed. By covetousness they will exploit you with deceptive words; for a long time their judgment has not been idle, and their destruction does not slumber.

What Did Jesus Say About Authority?

Hebrews 13:9 (NKJV)

Do not be carried about with various and strange doctrines. For *it is* good that the heart be established by grace, not with foods which have not profited those who have been occupied with them.

James 4:3–4 (NKJV)

You ask and do not receive, because you ask amiss, that you may spend *it* on your pleasures. Adulterers and adulteresses! Do you not know that friendship with the world is enmity with God? Whoever therefore wants to be a friend of the world makes himself an enemy of God.

1 John 4:1 (NKJV)

Beloved, do not believe every spirit, but test the spirits, whether they are of God; because many false prophets have gone out into the world.

2 Thessalonians 2:9–12 (NLT)

This man will come to do the work of Satan with counterfeit power and signs and miracles. He will use every kind of evil deception to fool those on their way to destruction, because they refuse to love and accept the truth that would save them. So God will cause them to be greatly deceived, and they will believe these lies. Then they will be condemned for enjoying evil rather than believing the truth.

While all of these warnings in Scripture about those who considered themselves authorities can be overwhelming, it is essential for our spiritual health and well-being that we take note of them. If we listen to false apostles, false prophets, and false teachers sent by Satan, but come in the name of the Lord and claim to represent God's authority, then they will separate us from God to follow false teachings and traditions of men. Most assuredly, they will not inform us if they are messengers from Satan. They may not even be aware of this deception because deceived people usually do not know they are deceived!

2 Corinthians 11:13–15 (NKJV)
For such *are* false apostles, deceitful workers, transforming themselves into apostles of Christ. And no wonder! For Satan himself transforms himself into an angel of light. Therefore *it is* no great thing if his ministers also transform themselves into ministers of righteousness, whose end will be according to their works.

2 Corinthians 4:4 (NLT)
Satan, who is the god of this world, has blinded the minds of those who don't believe. They are unable to see the glorious light of the Good News. They don't understand this message about the glory of Christ, who is the exact likeness of God.

The religious people in the days of Jesus Christ believed in their hearts they were serving God. They claimed to sit in the seat of Moses; they were sons of Abraham. They believed they were upholding the laws and commands of almighty God, passing judgment on people who did not submit to them, even putting those who believed in Jesus Christ out of the synagogues.

However, we know, from Christ's condemnation of them in Scripture, they were deceived and not doing God's will. Nor did they recognize the works of Jesus Christ as being of God. Yet, in their minds, they considered themselves authorities, established by God, and doing what they considered "the work of the Lord!"

So who are the real governing authorities in the body of Christ? How can we unquestionably identify the real authorities God established and avoid following the false leaders Jesus Christ warned us about in His Word?

Understanding the foundation and purpose for ministry appointed to the church by Jesus will help us to identify which authorities are doing the will of God.

Chapter 2

The Foundation
for Ministry

I have heard it often said, "Ministry begins in the local church." I certainly agree that most careers in ministry begin in the local church. However, getting involved in or getting people involved in church to do "works of ministry" is a false foundation for ministry.

In my research to understand the foundation and purpose for ministry, I looked to Jesus, the Head of the church, and the author of our faith. The foundation of Jesus Christ's ministry was in this passage of Scripture:

John 3:16–17(KJV)
> For God so loved the world, that he gave his
> only begotten Son, that whosoever believeth in
> him should not perish, but have everlasting
> life. For God sent not his Son into the world to
> condemn the world; but that the world through
> him might be saved.

What Did Jesus Say About Authority?

Here are a few more verses detailing Jesus Christ's ministry:

Luke 4:18 (NKJV)

"The Spirit of the Lord is upon Me,
Because He has anointed Me
To preach the gospel to the poor;
He has sent Me to heal the brokenhearted,
To proclaim liberty to the captives
And recovery of sight to the blind,
To set at liberty those who are oppressed."

John 10:9–16 (NKJV)

I am the door. If anyone enters by Me, he will be saved, and will go in and out and find pasture. The thief does not come except to steal, and to kill, and to destroy. I have come that they may have life, and that they may have *it* more abundantly.

"I am the good shepherd. The good shepherd gives His life for the sheep. But a hireling, *he who is* not the shepherd, one who does not own the sheep, sees the wolf coming and leaves the sheep and flees; and the wolf catches the sheep and scatters them. The hireling flees because he is a hireling and does not care about the sheep. I am the good shepherd; and I know My *sheep,* and am known by My own. As the Father knows Me, even so I know the Father; and I lay down My life for the sheep. And other sheep I have which are not of this fold; them also I must bring, and they will hear My voice; and there will be one flock *and* one shepherd."

What Did Jesus Say About Authority?

After the resurrection, before the ascension, as the disciples were hiding for fear of the Jews, Jesus appeared among them and said, "As the Father send me, so I sent you" (John 20:21).

Carrying out the "works of ministry" what Jesus came to do, bringing life to all humanity, and delivering humanity from the powers of darkness and turning them to God—this is the foundation for "works of ministry" in the church.

Scripture reveals, however, that it is possible to dedicate your life to "works of ministry" and end up in Hell!

Matthew 7:21–23 (NKJV)
"Not everyone who says to Me, 'Lord, Lord,' shall enter the kingdom of heaven, but he who does the will of My Father in heaven. Many will say to Me in that day, 'Lord, Lord, have we not prophesied in Your name, cast out demons in Your name, and done many wonders in Your name?' And then I will declare to them, 'I never knew you; depart from Me, you who practice lawlessness!'"

What a shock these people will receive as Jesus Christ turns them away from the pearly gates. They will claim they were doing "works of ministry" for Him in His Name. Nevertheless, Christ will turn them away because" They practiced lawlessness."

What Did Jesus Say About Authority?

How is it possible for the people who dedicated their lives to "works of ministry" to be turned away from the pearly gates by Jesus Christ because they were "practicing lawlessness?"

The Greek word used in this verse for lawlessness is "*anomia*"

From *Strong's Hebrew and Greek Dictionary*[5]:
G458
Anomia
Pronunciation: *an-om-ee'-ah*
From G459; *illegality*, that is, *violation of law* or (generally) *wickedness:*—iniquity, X transgress (-ion of) the law, unrighteousness.

From *Thayer's Greek Dictionary*:
1. the condition of without law
    1 a. because ignorant of it
    1 b. because of violating it
2. contempt and violation of law, iniquity, wickedness

As we look at an extreme example, the truth becomes clearer.

The elders and deacons of the Peoples Temple, for instance, did everything the founder of the movement, who claimed to be a man of God, asked them to do. To become deacons and elders, they had

---

[5]James Strong, *Strong's Hebrew and Greek Dictionaries* (Quick Verse, 2003), Electronic Edition STEP Files.

to submit to the vision of the founder, Jim Jones. Those elders and deacons who rightly challenged the founder's decisions were removed from their positions of authority and asked to leave. Some were so concerned about the welfare of the members of this religious community that they contacted their congressional representatives to investigate. When the investigation team arrived at the airport to help some members escape the community, they were ambushed, and some were killed.

These elders and deacons, who received their positions of authority in the Peoples Temple, by their actions, revealed they did not have the Biblical qualifications to be in authority. Instead, they received their authority because they submitted to the vision of the founder who claimed to be a man of God. Jones built his vision on this foundation:

Romans 13:1–2 (NKJV)
Let every soul be subject to the governing authorities. For there is no authority except from God, and the authorities that exist are appointed by God. Therefore whoever resists the authority resists the ordinance of God, and those who resist will bring judgment on themselves.

To avoid receiving judgment from the authority who claimed to be "God's authority," they submitted to Jones when he commanded them to serve the people—the very ones they were appointed to care for—poison and kill them!

What Did Jesus Say About Authority?

These elders and deacons made a horrific and tragic assumption. They assumed that Paul's teaching, an apostle of the church, in Romans 13:1–2 about submitting to authority, to avoid judgment, was more important than following the teaching of Jesus Christ, the Head of the Church, about honoring the first commandment—keeping God first in your life.

Let me be clear. When Paul said in Romans 13:1–2 that all authority is of God, and we must submit to them or face judgment, Paul never expected, nor taught, that we *violate the first commandment* to do so! Such an act would separate us from God and lead to our spiritual death. Paul and Jesus spoke against *violating the first commandment,* even in the face of judgment of death. Furthermore, Paul never implied that all authorities who claimed to be of God were following God. He said just the opposite: "Our battle is against rulers and authorities." In my studies, I found that in Romans 13:1–2 Paul used the same Greek word *exousia* to define the authorities that we are to submit to. Which Paul also used in Ephesians 6:12 to define the authorities that we, as Christians, fight against!

What was Paul thinking?

Why would Paul use the same Greek word *"exousia"* to define the authorities God created that we are to submit to in Romans 13:1–2, and the authorities our battle is against in Ephesians 6:12?

What Did Jesus Say About Authority?

What a horrific, deadly mistake, with eternal consequences this would be, if we submitted to the authorities *"exousia"* whom Paul says our battle is against. What a rude awaking we will have on judgment day as Christ turns us away from the pearly gates because we did "works of ministry," but failed to take the time learn or define the difference between the authorities *"exousia"* Paul said we are to submit to and the authorities *"exousia"* Paul said our battle is against. By then, it will be too late.

Now is the time to learn the difference between the power and authority ascribed by Scripture with the same Greek word *exousia*[G1849] to both God's kingdom and Satan's kingdom.[6]

Returning to the elders and deacons of the Peoples Temple; although they were following the principles in Romans 13:1–2, submitting to and doing everything asked of them by the one who claimed to be the authority in their life, to avoid judgment, they were practicing lawlessness. They not only violated but also led their people to violate the most important law in the Bible: *honoring the first commandment!* By putting the will of the authority in their lives above and before the foundation and purpose of Christ's ministry He

---

[6] For an in-depth discussion of these two kingdoms, visit www.ourgodgivenrights.com. to download a free PDF copy or purchase a print edition of my previous book *OUR GOD-GIVEN RIGHTS: To the Fullness of Our Salvation & the Vast Demonic Conspiracy.*

appointed to the church, which was to give life, they led over 900 people to their death! And they lost their own lives as well! They had sold out to do "works of ministry" for the vision of the authority in their lives. However, they were not committed to the foundational purpose for ministry appointed to the church by Jesus Christ!

This horrible, tragic event can teach us many lessons about submitting to authority, something these elders and deacons did. Looking at this objectively will expose and demolish many assumptions we have about authority in the church.

The actions of many, but not all, ministries under which I have served, revealed the foundation of their ministry to be based on Romans 13:1–2, instead of the foundation and purpose for ministry Jesus appointed to the church. If you did not submit to doing what was asked, even after being so tired and burned out that you could not function, you were judged and condemned. Such happened even though Christ's appointed purpose for ministry was to give life and not to condemn as stated in John 3:16–17.

They also promoted people to positions of authority because they submitted to the vision and perceived authority of those who claimed to be authorities rather than according to the qualification listed in Scripture to receive authority in the church. This false foundation for ministry was built on exalted self-seeking, charming people who cared more about themselves and their careers in ministry than those they were appointed to serve. Lacking this Biblical foundation for ministry, they dominated, controlled, and ruled over those they were appointed to serve. They did so in violation of Christ's teaching—that such worldly expression of authority does not belong among His people.

This "work of ministry" caused devastation and destruction in the lives of many people I knew and cared for, including mine. Yet, no one would address the abuse of authority, as no one would hear anything negative said about this or that person because they were in a position of authority. Such denial kept the door open for more lives to be destroyed. It also meant no one could or would be held accountable to follow and maintain the qualifications and purpose for ministry Jesus Christ established in His church, which forced their victims to leave the church to end such mistreatment.

These inactions also rejected applying God's wisdom to the situation as defined in James 3:17 and hindered Christ's reconciliation, healing, and deliverance ministry in the church. The victims were forced to look elsewhere for healing and relief from the pain. Furthermore, by refusing to address the abuse and misuse of authority in the church, these authorities implied that the message of the gospel—which tells the whole world to repent of its sin and live righteous holy lives before God—does not apply to the leaders in the church.

What Did Jesus Say About Authority?

The qualifications in Scripture to receive authority in the church are as follows:[7]

Titus 1:5–9

1. Above reproach
    Not open to censure; having unimpeachable integrity
2. Husband of one wife
    (A one-wife kind of man, not a philanderer; Does not necessarily rule out widowers or divorced men)
3. Having believing children
    (children are Christians, not incorrigible or unruly)
4. Not self-willed
    Not arrogantly self-satisfied
5. Not quick-tempered
    Not prone to anger or irascible
6. Not addicted to wine
    Not fond of wine or drunk
7. Not pugnacious
    Not contentious or quarrelsome
8. Not a money-lover
    Not greedy for money
9. Hospitable
    A stranger-lover, generous to guests
10. Lover of good
    Loving goodness
11. Sensible
    Self-controlled, sane, temperate

---

[7] This list is taken from Lawrence O. Richards, *A Theology of Church Leadership* (Zondervan, 1980).

12. Just
    Righteous, upright, aligned with right
13. Devout
    Responsible in fulfilling moral obligations to
    God and man
14. Self-controlled
    Restrained, under control
15. Holding fast the Word
    Committed to God's Word as authoritative
16. Able to teach sound doctrine
    Calling others to wholeness through teaching
    God's Word
17. Able to refute objections
    Convincing those who speak against the truth

Additional from 1 Timothy 3:1–7

18. Temperate
    Calm and collected in spirit; sober
19. Gentle
    Fair, equitable, not insisting on his own rights
20. Able to manage household
    A good leader in his own family
21. Not a new convert
    Not a new Christian
22. Well thought of
    A good representative of Christ

Additional from 1 Peter 5:1–4

23. Serves willingly, not under compulsion
    Not serving against his will
24. According to God (in some Greek texts)
    By God's appointment
25. Not for shameful gain

Not motivated by money
26. Not lording it over the flock
    Not dominating in his area of ministry (a
    shepherd should lead, not drive, the flock)
27. As an example
    A pleasure to follow because of his Christian
    example
28. As accountable to the Chief Shepherd
    Motivated by the crown to be gained(i.e.,
    authority to reign with Christ)

Did you notice? Submitting to authority to get authority in the church is not listed as a qualification for promotion to a position of authority in the church. Nor does Scripture say anything about submitting to the vision of the authority to get authority. If you look closely, the qualifications for receiving authority in the church are all about character and motives of the heart to do the "works of ministry" the Father sent Jesus to do, and Jesus now sends the church to do.

In the Bible, submitting to authority to get authority is a principal promised by the devil, *not* Jesus!

Luke 4:5–7 (NKJV)
    Then the devil took him up and revealed to him
    all the kingdoms of the world in a moment of
    time. "I will give you the glory of these
    kingdoms and authority over them," the devil
    said, "because they are mine to give to anyone I
    please. I will give it all to you if you will
    worship me."

What Did Jesus Say About Authority?

> Jesus replied, "The Scriptures say,
>
> 'You must worship the LORD your God and serve only him.'"

Jesus Christ gave us authority because of our belief in Him as our Lord and Savior. This authority is a gift; it is never earned. He did not give everyone authority to run administrative affairs in the church, which is by qualifications of character and motives of the heart as listed in Scripture, but, He gave everyone authority to overcome the powers of darkness that are trying to separate us from God, so they can destroy us.

Luke 10:19-20 (NKJV)
> "Behold, I give you the authority to trample on serpents and scorpions, and over all the power of the enemy, and nothing shall by any means hurt you. Nevertheless do not rejoice in this, that the spirits are subject to you, but rather rejoice because your names are written in heaven."

The "works of ministry" performed by the elders and deacons of the Peoples Temple concerned serving a man, not God. They got their authority from man, not God. They served death, not life. They led the people to follow the vision of a man, violate the first commandment, which separated them from God. Rather than, reconcile them to God, the foundation and purpose of Christ's ministry, which He appointed to the church. In all of this, they followed the principles found in Romans 13:1–

2.They were obedient to, submitted to, and served the vision of the one who claimed to be "God's delegated authority," to avoid the judgment of the authority, Jim Jones. None of these "works of ministry" was for *JESUS CHRIST, the purpose of His ministry, or His people's welfare!* They promoted violating and rebelling against the most important law in the Bible: "honoring the first commandment." This was the very thing the Serpent did to Adam and Eve.

As I have watched the rise of Marxism in America, I have observed something very alarming. Marxism has been building its vision on the principles found in Romans 13:1–2. If people do not submit to Marxism's vision/authority, they will be, judged, condemned, destroyed, and killed. The graves of millions in countries that have succumbed to Marxism testify to this. Marxism always has and always will judge, condemn, and destroy the lives of those who do not submit to its vision/authority.

I observed ISIS attempt to build its kingdom on the same principles found in Romans 13:1–2. ISIS judged, condemned and beheaded 21 men in orange jump suits on live television because they refused to violate the first command, denounce Jesus, and submit the vision and perceived authority of ISIS.

Likewise, the Bible says, the Beast, who is the ultimate manifestation of the spirit of the anti-christ, will establish his kingdom on the same principles found in Romans 13:1–2. Anyone who does not submit to his authority and take his number will be judged, condemned, and put to death (Rev. 13.).

Besides building their organizations on the principles found in Romans 13:1–2, giving authority to those who submit to their vision, and condemning and destroying those who do not submit, these religious cults, Marxism, ISIS, and the Beast have another thing in common. They do *not* acknowledge, honor, and respect the God-given rights, authority, and freedoms of the New Covenant believer Jesus Christ bestowed upon them with their precious gift of salvation![8] Thus, they deny and reject the redemptive work of Jesus Christ on the cross—the foundation and purpose for the ministry appointed to the church by Jesus Christ Himself!

No born-again believer is required by God to submit to those who deny Jesus Christ's redemptive work, even if they claim to be authorities and have the power to condemn. Instead, our battle is against them (Eph. 6:12). After all, Jesus Christ said, "the most important thing to do in the Bible is to *honor the first commandment*." Getting people to violate God's commands, including the first commandment, is promoting, partnering with, and practicing lawlessness. Regarding the people who do this, Jesus said, "He will turn them away from the pearly gates, even if they were doing 'works of ministry' in His Name" (Matt. 7:21–23).

---

[8] To learn more about *OUR GOD-GIVEN RIGHTS*, visit www.ourgodgivenrights.com.

What Did Jesus Say About Authority?

What really matters is the authority of Jesus Christ the head of the church. He tells us, *"Honoring the first commandment is the most important thing to do."* His servants will *in no way* lead us against that.

There is *never* any Biblical justification for getting people to *violate the first commandment* in an effort to get them to commit to or follow anything else. That is purely leading people in rebellion against, and separating them, from God, which will lead to their spiritual death! Such "works of ministry" are just the opposite of the foundation and purpose for ministry appointed to the church by Jesus Christ, which is to give life.

Chapter 3

Identifying Authority

King James Version
The word authority (ies) appears 36 times in 33 verses. It translates from seven Greek words.

New King James Version
The word authority (ies) appears 73 times in 67 verses. It translates from 12 Greek words.

New Living Translation
The word authority (ies) appears 126 times in 113 verses. The *New Living Translation* of the Bible adds the word authority in many verses where the word authority does not appear in other translations of the Bible (as does the *New International Version*). It, therefore, is impossible to determine which Greek word authority translates from.

What Did Jesus Say About Authority?

Greek words in the New Testament "authority" translates from.

	KJV	NKJV
Exousia [G1849]	29 times	53 times
Katexousiazo [G2715]	2 times	2 times
Exousiazo [G1850]	1 time	3 times
Dunastes [G1413]	1 time	1 time
Huperuche [G5247]	1 time	1 time
Authenteo [G831]	1 time	1 time
Epitage [G2003]	1 time	1 time
Emautou/emauto/emauton [G1683]		3 times
Heautou [G1438]		2 times
Archon [G758]		1 time
Dunatos [G1415]		1 time
Kuriotes [G2963]		2 times

What Did Jesus Say About Authority?

Exousia[G1849] is the Greek word most often translated as authority. It appears 103 times in 93 verses.
It translates into these English words in the Scripture verses, as illustrated in Chapters 5–7:

	KJV	**NKJV**
Authority (ies)	29 times	53 times
Power (s)	69 times	38 times
Rights (s)	2 times	8 times
Liberty	1 time	1 time
Jurisdiction	1 time	1 time
Strength	1 time	--
Control	--	1 time

What Did Jesus Say About Authority?

Exousia^{G1849} defines, expresses, and identifies the power, authority, and/or rights of:

- God,
- Jesus Christ,
- Apostles,
- Disciples,
- Believers,
- Angels, and
- Civil and religious governments.

Similarly, the word also defines, expresses, and identifies the power and/or authority of:

- Satan,
- The devil,
- The Beast,
- The Dragon,
- Scorpions,
- Serpents, and
- The kingdom and power of darkness.

What Did Jesus Say About Authority?

The next six chapters of this book contain every verse where the previously mentioned Greek words appear in the Bible and sometimes translate as authority, in three translations of the Bible (KJV, NKJV, and NLT) for easy comparison.

Order of Study

1. The Greek word from which authority translates.
2. *Strong's Hebrew and Greek Dictionary* number and Greek definition.
3. *Thayer's Greek Dictionary* definition.
4. Two lists: all English words into which each Greek word is translated and all the verses where that Greek word appears in the Bible.
5. Every time that word appears in the three translations of the Bible for easy comparison.
6. The King James Version with the English translation of the Greek word underlined and bold. The numbers identify the Greek words in *Strong's Exhaustive Concordance* from which the English words are translated.
7. The *New King James Version*
8. The *New Living Translation*
9. As I used only the verses where the Greek word that translates as authority appears, read the verses before and after to get a complete understanding of the passage.

Chapter 4

Authority
of This
World

As Defined
by
Jesus Christ

Jesus Christ used four words in three verses of the Bible to define authority of this world that does not belong among His people. Those four words—*katakurieuo*[G2634],*katexousiazo*[G2715], *kurieuo*[G296], exousiazo[G1850]—appear below along with their definitions from *Strong's Hebrew and Greek Dictionary* and *Thayer's Greek Dictionary* every time those words appear in the Bible.

Katakurieuo

G2634
katakurieuo
Pronunciation: *kat-ak-oo-ree-yoo'-o*

What Did Jesus Say About Authority?

From G2596 and G2961 in *Strong's Hebrew and Greek Dictionary*: to *lord against*; that is, *control, subjugate:*—exercise dominion over (lordship), be lord over, overcome.

From *Thayer's Greek Dictionary*:
1. to bring under one's power, to subject one's self, to subdue, master
2. to hold in subjection, to be master of, exercise lordship over

Part of speech: verb

Total KJV Occurrences: 8

Translated as follows:
exercise, 2
Matt. 20:25; Mark 10:42
lords, 2
1 Pet. 5:3; Rev. 17:14
dominion, 1
Matt. 20:25
lordship, 1
Mark 10:42
over, 1
1 Pet. 5:3
overcame, 1
Acts 19:16

Matthew 20:25
KJV
But Jesus G2424 called G4341 them unto him, and

said [G2036], Ye know [G1492] that the princes [G758] of the Gentiles [G1484] **exercise**[G2634] **dominion**[G2634] over them, and they that are great [G3171] exercise [G2715] authority [G2715] upon them.

NKJV

> But Jesus called them to *Himself* and said, "You know that the rulers of the Gentiles lord it over them, and those who are great exercise authority over them.

NLT

> But Jesus called them together and said, "You know that the rulers in this world lord it over their people, and officials flaunt their authority over those under them.

Mark 10:42

KJV

> But Jesus [G2424] called [G4341] them to him, and saith [G3004] unto them, Ye know [G1492] that they which are accounted [G1380] to rule [G757] over the Gentiles[G1484] **exercise**[G2634] **lordship**[G2634] over them; and their great [G3173] ones exercise [G2715] authority [G2715] upon them.

NKJV

> But Jesus called them to *Himself* and said to them, "You know that those who are considered rulers over the Gentiles lord it over them, and their great ones exercise authority over them.

NLT

> So Jesus called them together and said, "You know that the rulers in this world lord it over their people, and officials flaunt their authority over those under them.

Acts 19:16

KJV

> And the man [G444] in whom [G3739] the evil [G4190] spirit [G4151] was leaped [G2177] on [G1909] them, and **overcame**[G2634] them, and prevailed [G2480] against [G2596] them, so [G5620] that they fled [G1628] out of that house [G3624] naked [G1131] and wounded [G5135].

NKJV

> Then the man in whom the evil spirit was leaped on them, overpowered them, and prevailed against them, so that they fled out of that house naked and wounded.

NLT

> Then the man with the evil spirit leaped on them, overpowered them, and attacked them with such violence that they fled from the house, naked and battered.

1 Peter 5:3

KJV

> Neither [G3366] as being **lords**[G2634] **over**[G2634] God's [G2316] heritage [G2819], but being [G1096] ensamples [G5179] to the flock [G4168].

NKJV

nor as being lords over those entrusted to you,
but being examples to the flock;

NLT

Don't lord it over the people assigned to your
care, but lead them by your own good example.

Revelations 17:14
KJV

These [G3778] shall make [G4170] war [G4170] with the
Lamb [G721], and the Lamb [G721] shall overcome
[G3528] them: for he is Lord [G2962]**of lords**[G2634], and
King [G935] of kings [G935]: and they that are with
him are called [G2822], and chosen [G1588], and
faithful [G4103].

NKJV

These will make war with the Lamb, and the
Lamb will overcome them, for He is Lord of
lords and King of kings; and those *who are* with
Him *are* called, chosen, and faithful."

NLT

Together they will go to war against the Lamb,
but the Lamb will defeat them because he is Lord
of all lords and King of all kings. And his called
and chosen and faithful ones will be with him."

Katexousiazo

G2715
katexousiazo
Pronunciation: *kat-ex-oo-see-ad'-zo*

What Did Jesus Say About Authority?

From G2596 and G1850 in *Strong's Hebrew and Greek Dictionary*: to *have (wield) full privilege over:*—exercise authority.

From *Thayer's Greek Dictionary*
   1. to exercise authority, wield power

Part of speech: verb

Total KJV Occurrences:4

Translated as follows:
authority, 2
Matt. 20:24;Mark 10:42
exercise, 2
Matt. 20:25; Mark 10:42

Matthew 20:25
KJV
   But Jesus [G2424] called [G4341] them unto him, and said [G2036], Ye know [G1492] that the princes [G758] of the Gentiles [G1484] exercise [G2634] dominion [G2634] over them, and they that are great [G3171]**exercise** [G2715]**authority**[G2715]upon them.

NKJV
   But Jesus called them to *Himself* and said, "You know that the rulers of the Gentiles lord it over them, and those who are great exercise authority over them.

NLT
   But Jesus called them together and said, "You

know that the rulers in this world lord it over their people, and officials flaunt their authority over those under them."

Mark 10:42

KJV

But Jesus [G2424] called [G4341] them to him, and saith [G3004] unto them, Ye know [G1492] that they which are accounted [G1380] to rule [G757] over the Gentiles [G1484] exercise [G2634] lordship [G2634] over them; and their great [G3173] ones **exercise**[G2715]**authority**[G2715]upon them.

NKJV

But Jesus called them to *Himself* and said to them, "You know that those who are considered rulers over the Gentiles lord it over them, and their great ones exercise authority over them.

NLT

So Jesus called them together and said, "You know that the rulers in this world lord it over their people, and officials flaunt their authority over those under them.

Kurieuo

G2961

kurieuo

Pronunciation: *koo-ree-yoo'-o*

From G2962*Strong's Hebrew and Greek Dictionary*: to *rule:*—have dominion over, lord, be lord of, exercise lordship over.

What Did Jesus Say About Authority?

From *Thayer's Greek Dictionary*:
1. to be lord of, to rule, have dominion over
2. of things and forces
2a. to exercise influence upon, to have power over

Part of speech: verb

Total KJV Occurrences: 8

Translated as follows:
dominion, 4
Rom 6:9, Rom 6:14, Rom 7:1, 2 Cor. 1:24
exercise, 1
Luke 22:24
lord, 1
Rom. 14:9
lords, 1
1 Tim. 6:15
lordship, 1
Luke 22:25

Luke 22:25
KJV
> And he said [G2036] unto them, The kings [G935] of the Gentiles [G1484]**exercise**[G2961] **lordship**[G2961] over them; and they that exercise [G1850] authority [G1850] upon them are called [G2564] benefactors [G2110].

NKJV
> And He said to them, "The kings of the Gentiles exercise lordship over them, and those who

exercise authority over them are called 'benefactors.'"

NLT

Jesus told them, "In this world the kings and great men lord it over their people, yet they are called 'friends of the people.'"

Romans 6:9

KJV

Knowing [G1492] that Christ [G5547] being raised [G1453] from the dead [G3498] dieth [G599] no [G3765] more [G2089]; death [G2288] hath no [G3765] more [G3765] **dominion** [G2961] over him.

NKJV

Knowing that Christ, having been raised from the dead, dies no more. Death no longer has dominion over Him.

NLT

We are sure of this because Christ was raised from the dead, and he will never die again. Death no longer has any power over him.

Romans 6:14

KJV

For sin [G266] shall not have **dominion**[G2961] over you: for ye are not under [G5259] the law [G3551], but under [G5259] grace [G5485].

NKJV

For sin shall not have dominion over you, for

you are not under law but under grace.

NLT

Sin is no longer your master, for you no longer live under the requirements of the law. Instead, you live under the freedom of God's grace.

Romans 7:1

KJV

Know [G50] ye not, brethren [G80], (for I speak [G2980] to them that know [G1097] the law [G3551]) how that the law [G3551] hath **dominion**[G2961] over a man [G444] as long [G5550] as he liveth [G2198]?

NKJV

Or do you not know, brethren (for I speak to those who know the law), that the law has dominion over a man as long as he lives?

NLT

Now, dear brothers and sisters you who are familiar with the law—don't you know that the law applies only while a person is living?

Romans 14:9

KJV

For to this [G5124] end Christ [G5547] both [G2532] died [G599], and rose [G450], and revived [G326], that he might be **Lord**[G2961] both [G2532] of the dead [G3498] and living [G2198].

NKJV

For to this end Christ died and rose and lived

again, that He might be Lord of both the dead and the living.

NLT

Christ died and rose again for this very purpose—to be Lord both of the living and of the dead.

2 Corinthians 1:24
KJV

Not for that we have **dominion** G2961 over your G5216 faith G4102, but are helpers G4904 of your G5216 joy G5479: for by faith G4102 ye stand G2476.

NKJV

Not that we have dominion over your faith, but are fellow workers for your joy; for by faith you stand.

NLT

But that does not mean we want to dominate you by telling you how to put your faith into practice. We want to work together with you so you will be full of joy, for it is by your own faith that you stand firm.

1 Timothy 6:15
KJV

Which G3739 in his times G5550 he shall show G1166, who G3588 is the blessed G3107 and only G3441 Potentate G1413, the King G935 of kings G936, and Lord G2962 of **lords** G2961.

NKJV

> which He will manifest in His own time, *He who is* the blessed and only Potentate, the King of kings and Lord of lords,

NLT

> For at just the right time Christ will be revealed from heaven by the blessed and only almighty God, the King of all kings and Lord of all lords.

Exousiazo

G1850

exousiazo
Pronunciation: *ex-oo-see-ad'-zo*
From G1849*Strong's Hebrew and Greek Dictionary*: to *control:*—exercise authority upon, bring under the (have) power of.

From *Thayer's Greek Dictionary*:
1.   to have power or authority, use power
1a.   to be master of any one, exercise authority over one
1b. to be master of the body
1b1. to have full and entire authority over the body
1b2.to hold the body subject to one's will
1c.to be brought under the power of anyone

Part of Speech: verb

Total KJV Occurrences: 6

What Did Jesus Say About Authority?

Translated as follows:
power, 3
1 Cor. 6:12; 1 Cor. 7:4 (2)
authority, 1
Luke 22:25
brought, 1
1 Cor. 6:12
exercise, 1
Luke 22:25

Luke 22:25
KJV

And he said ^{G2036} unto them, The kings ^{G935} of the Gentiles ^{G1484} exercise ^{G2961} lordship ^{G2961} over them; and they that **exercise**^{G1850} **authority** ^{G1850} upon them are called ^{G2564} benefactors ^{G2110}.

NKJV

And He said to them, "The kings of the Gentiles exercise lordship over them, and those who exercise authority over them are called 'benefactors.'

NLT

Jesus told them, "In this world the kings and great men lord it over their people, yet they are called 'friends of the people.'"

1 Corinthians 6:12
KJV

All ^{G3956} things are lawful ^{G1832} unto me, but all ^{G3956} things are not expedient ^{G4851}: all ^{G3956} things are lawful ^{G1832} for me, but I will not be

brought[G1850] under [G5259]**the power**[G1850] of any [G5100].

NKJV

All things are lawful for me, but all things are not helpful. All things are lawful for me, but I will not be brought under the power of any.

NLT

You say, "I am allowed to do anything"—but not everything is good for you. And even though "I am allowed to do anything," I must not become a slave to anything.

1 Corinthians 7:4

KJV

The wife [G1135] hath not **power**[G1850] of her own [G2398] body [G4983], but the husband [G435]: and likewise [G3668] also [G2532] the husband [G435] hath not **power**[G1850] of his own [G2398] body [G4983], but the wife [G1135].

NKJV

The wife does not have authority over her own body, but the husband *does*. And likewise the husband does not have authority over his own body, but the wife *does*.

NLT

The wife gives authority over her body to her husband, and the husband gives authority over his body to his wife.

Chapter 5

Authority, God's Kingdom of Light

In the following Scripture verses, Exousia identifies:

The power and authority of God (6)

The power and authority of Christ/Son of Man (17)

The power and authority of disciples (5)

The power, authority and rights of servants /believers (11)

The power, authority and rights of apostles (11)

The power and authority of angels (2)

The power of two witnesses (2)

Greek definitions from Strong's and Thayer's dictionaries

G1849

εξουσία

exousia

pronunciation: *ex-oo-see'-ah*

From G1832 (in the sense of *ability*); *privilege,* that is, (subjectively) *force, capacity, competency, freedom,* or (objectively) *mastery* (concretely *magistrate, superhuman, potentate, tokenofcontrol*), delegated *influence:*—authority, jurisdiction, liberty, power, right, strength.

Thayer's Greek Dictionary:

1) power of choice, liberty of doing as one pleases

1a) leave or permission

2) physical and mental power

2a) the ability or strength with which one is endued, which he either possesses or exercises

3) the power of authority (influence) and of right (privilege)

4) the power of rule or government (the power of him whose will and commands must be submitted to by others and obeyed)

4a) universally

4a1) authority over mankind

4b) specifically

4b1) the power of judicial decisions

4b2) of authority to manage domestic affairs

4c) metonymically
4c1) a thing subject to authority or rule
4c1a) jurisdiction
4c2) one who possesses authority
4c2a) a ruler, a human magistrate
4c2b) the leading and more powerful among created beings superior to man, spiritual potentates
4d) a sign of the husband's authority over his wife
4d1) the veil with which propriety required a women to cover herself
4e) the sign of regal authority, a crown

Part of Speech: noun feminine

Total KJV Occurrences 103

Translated as follows:
power, 61
Matt. 9:6; Matt. 9:8; Matt. 10:1; Matt. 28:18; Mark 2:10; Mark 3:15; Mark 6:7; Luke 4:6; Luke 4:32; Luke 5:24; Luke 10:19; Luke 12:5; Luke 22:53; John 1:12; John 10:18 (2); John 17:2; John 19:10–11 (3); Acts 1:7; Acts 5:4; Acts 8:19; Acts 26:18; Rom. 9:21; Rom. 13:1–3 (3); 1 Cor. 7:37; 1 Cor. 9:4–6 (3); 1 Cor. 9:12 (2); 1 Cor. 9:18; 1 Cor. 11:10; 2 Cor. 13:10; Eph. 1:21; Eph. 2:2; Col. 1:13; Col. 2:10; 2 Thess. 3:9; Rev. 2:25–26 (2); Rev. 6:8; Rev. 9:3 (2); Rev. 9:10; Rev. 9:19; Rev. 11:6 (2); Rev. 12:10; Rev. 13:4–5 (2); Rev. 13:7; Rev. 13:12; Rev. 14:18; Rev. 16:9; Rev. 17:12; Rev. 18:1; Rev. 20:6

authority, 28
Matt. 7:29; Matt. 8:9; Matt. 21:23–24 (3); Matt. 21:27; Mark 1:22; Mark 11:27–29 (4); Mark 13:33–34 (2); Luke 4:36; Luke 7:8; Luke 9:1; Luke 19:17; Luke 20:2 (2); Luke 20:8; Luke 20:20; John 5:27; Acts 9:14; Acts 26:10; Acts 26:12; 1 Cor. 15:24; 2 Cor. 10:8; Rev 13:2

powers, 8
Luke 12:11; Rom. 13:1 (2); Eph. 3:10; Eph. 6:12; Col. 1:16; Col. 2:15, Titus 3:1

right, 2
Heb. 13:10; Rev. 22:14

authorities, 1
1 Pet. 3:22

jurisdiction, 1
Luke 23:7

liberty, 1
1 Cor. 8:9

strength, 1
Rev. 17:13

The power and authority of God (6)

Luke 12:5
KJV

But I will forewarn G5263 you whom G5101 ye shall fear G5399: Fear G5399 him, which after G3326 he hath killed G615 hath G2192**power G1849** to cast G1685 into G1519 hell G1067; yea G3483, I say G3004 unto you, Fear G5399 him.

NKJV

But I will show you whom you should fear: Fear

Him who, after He has killed, has power to cast
into hell; yes, I say to you, fear Him!

NLT

But I'll tell you whom to fear. Fear God, who
has the power to kill you and then throw you into
hell. Yes, he's the one to fear.

John 19:11
KJV

Jesus [G2424] answered [G611], Thou couldest have
[G2192] no [G3756]**power[G1849]** at all [G3762] against [G2596]
me, except [G1508] it were given [G1325] thee from
above [G509]: therefore [G1223_G5124] he that delivered
[G3860] me unto thee hath [G2192] the greater [G3187] sin
[G266].

NKJV

Jesus answered, "You could have no power at all
against Me unless it had been given you from
above. Therefore the one who delivered Me to
you has the greater sin."

NLT

Then Jesus said, "You would have no power
over me at all unless it were given to you from
above. So the one who handed me over to you
has the greater sin."

Acts 1:7
KJV

And he said [G2036] unto them, It is not for you to
know [G1097] the times [G5550] or [G2228] the seasons

G2540, which G3739 the Father G3962 hath put G5087 in his own G2398 **power**G1849.

NKJV

And He said to them, "It is not for you to know times or seasons which the Father has put in His own authority.

NLT

He replied, "The Father alone has the authority to set those dates and times, and they are not for you to know.

Romans 9:21

KJV

Hath G2192 not the potter G2763 **power**G1849 over the clay G4081, of the same G846 lump G5445 to make G4160 one vessel G4632 unto honour G5092, and another G3739 unto dishonor G819?

NKJV

Does not the potter have power over the clay, from the same lump to make one vessel for honor and another for dishonor?

NLT

When a potter makes jars out of clay, doesn't he have a right to use the same lump of clay to make one jar for decoration and another to throw garbage into?

Jude 1:25

KJV

To the only [G3441] wise [G4680] God [G2316] our Saviour [G4990], be glory [G1391] and majesty [G3172], dominion [G2904] and **power**[G1849], both [G2532] now [G3568] and for ever [G3956_G165]. Amen [G281].

NKJV

To God our Savior, Who alone is wise, *Be* glory and majesty, Dominion and power, Both now and forever. Amen.

NLT

All glory to him who alone is God, our Savior through Jesus Christ our Lord. All glory, majesty, power, and authority are his before all time, and in the present, and beyond all time! Amen.

Revelations 16:9

KJV

And men [G444] were scorched [G2739] with great [G3173] heat [G2738], and blasphemed [G987] the name [G3686] of God [G2316], which [G3588] hath [G2192]**power G1849** over [G1909] these [G5025] plagues [G4127]: and they repented [G3340] not to give [G1325] him glory [G1391].

NKJV

And men were scorched with great heat, and they blasphemed the name of God who has power over these plagues; and they did not repent and give Him glory.

NLT

Everyone was burned by this blast of heat, and

they cursed the name of God, who had control over all these plagues. They did not repent of their sins and turn to God and give him glory.

The power and authority of Christ/Son of Man (17)

Matthew 7:29
KJV

For he taught [G2258_G1321] them as one having [G2192]**authority** **G1849**, and not as the scribes [G1122].

NKJV

for He taught them as one having authority, and not as the scribes.

NLT

for he taught with real authority—quite unlike their teachers of religious law.

Mathew 9:6
KJV

But that ye may know [G1492] that the Son [G5207] of man [G444] hath [G2192]**power** **G1849** on [G1909] earth [G1093] to forgive [G863] sins [G266], (then [G5119] saith [G3004] he to the sick [G3885] of the palsy [G3885],) Arise [G1453], take [G142] up thy bed [G2825], and go [G5217] unto thine [G4675] house [G3624].

NKJV

But that you may know that the Son of Man has power on earth to forgive sins"—then He said to the paralytic, "Arise, take up your bed, and go to your house."

NLT

So I will prove to you that the Son of Man has the authority on earth to forgive sins." Then Jesus turned to the paralyzed man and said, "Stand up, pick up your mat, and go home!"

Matthew 9:8

KJV

But when the multitude G3793 saw G1492 it, they marvelled G2296, and glorified G1392 God G2316, which G3588 had given G1325 such G5108**power G1849**unto men G444.

NKJV

Now when the multitudes saw *it,* they marveled and glorified God, who had given such power to men.

NLT

Fear swept through the crowd as they saw this happen. And they praised God for sending a man with such great authority.

Matt 28:18

KJV

And Jesus G2424 came G4334 and spake G2980 unto them, saying G3004, All G3956**power**G1849 is given G1325 unto me in heaven G3772 and in earth G1093.

NKJV

And Jesus came and spoke to them, saying, "All

authority has been given to Me in heaven and on earth.

NLT

Jesus came and told his disciples, "I have been given all authority in heaven and on earth.

Mark 1:22

KJV

And they were astonished [G1605] at [G1909] his doctrine [G1322]: for he taught [G2258]_[G1321] them as one that had [G2192]**authority**[G1849], and not as the scribes [G1122].

NKJV

And they were astonished at His teaching, for He taught them as one having authority, and not as the scribes.

NLT

The people were amazed at his teaching, for he taught with real authority—quite unlike the teachers of religious law.

Mark 1:27

KJV

And they were all [G3956] amazed [G2284], insomuch [G5620] that they questioned [G4802] among [G4314] themselves [G848], saying [G3004], What [G5101] thing is this [G3778]? What [G5101] new [G2537] doctrine [G1322] is this [G5124]? for with **authority**[G1849] commandeth [G2004] he even [G2532] the unclean [G169] spirits [G4151], and they do obey [G5219] him.

What Did Jesus Say About Authority?

NKJV

Then they were all amazed, so that they
questioned among themselves, saying, "What is
this? What new doctrine *is* this? For with
authority He commands even the unclean spirits,
and they obey Him."

NLT

Amazement gripped the audience, and they
began to discuss what had happened. "What sort
of new teaching is this?" they asked excitedly.
"It has such authority! Even evil spirits obey his
orders!"

Mark 2:10

KJV

But that ye may know [G1492] that the Son [G5207] of
man [G444] hath [G2192]**power**[G1849] on [G1909] earth [G1093]
to forgive [G863] sins [G266], (he saith [G3004] to the sick
[G3885] of the palsy [G3885],)

NKJV

But that you may know that the Son of Man has
power on earth to forgive sins"—He said to the
paralytic,

NLT

So I will prove to you that the Son of Man has
the authority on earth to forgive sins." Then
Jesus turned to the paralyzed man and said,

Luke 4:32

What Did Jesus Say About Authority?

KJV

> And they were astonished ^{G1605} at ^{G1909} his doctrine ^{G1322}: for his word G3056 was with **power** ^{G1849}.

NKJV

> And they were astonished at His teaching, for His word was with authority.

NLT

> There, too, the people were amazed at his teaching, for he spoke with authority

Luke 4:36

KJV

> And they were all ^{G3956} amazed $^{G1096\_G2285}$, and spake ^{G4814} among ^{G4314} themselves ^{G240}, saying ^{G3004}, What ^{G5101} a word ^{G3056} is this ^{G3778}! for with **authority**^{G1849} and power ^{G1411} he commandeth ^{G2004} the unclean ^{G169} spirits ^{G4151}, and they come ^{G1831} out.

NKJV

> Then they were all amazed and spoke among themselves, saying, "What a word this *is!* For with authority and power He commands the unclean spirits, and they come out.

NLT

> Amazed, the people exclaimed, "What authority and power this man's words possess! Even evil spirits obey him, and they flee at his command!

What Did Jesus Say About Authority?

Luke 5:24
KJV

> But that ye may know ^{G1492} that the Son ^{G5207} of man ^{G444} hath ^{G2192}**power**^{G1849} upon earth ^{G1093} to forgive ^{G863} sins ^{G266}, (he said ^{G2036} unto the sick ^{G3885} of the palsy ^{G3886},) I say ^{G3004} unto thee, Arise ^{G1453}, and take ^{G142} up thy couch ^{G2826}, and go ^{G4198} into ^{G1519} thine ^{G4675} house ^{G3624}.

NKJV

> But that you may know that the Son of Man has power on earth to forgive sins"—He said to the man who was paralyzed, "I say to you, arise, take up your bed, and go to your house."

NLT

> So I will prove to you that the Son of Man has the authority on earth to forgive sins." Then Jesus turned to the paralyzed man and said, "Stand up, pick up your mat, and go home!"

John 5:27
KJV

> And hath given ^{G1325} him **authority**^{G1849} to execute ^{G4160} judgment ^{G2920} also ^{G2532}, because ^{G3754} he is the Son ^{G5207} of man ^{G444}.

NKJV

> and has given Him authority to execute judgment also, because He is the Son of Man.

NLT

> And he has given him authority to judge

everyone because he is the Son of Man.

John 10:18
KJV

No [G3762] man [G3762] taketh [G142] it from me, but I lay [G5087] it down of myself [G1683]. I have [G2192] **power**[G1849] to lay [G5087] it down, and I have [G2192] **power**[G1849] to take [G2983] it again [G3825]. This [G5026] commandment [G1785] have [G2192] I received [G2983] of my Father [G3962].

NKJV

No one takes it from Me, but I lay it down of Myself. I have power to lay it down, and I have power to take it again. This command I have received from My Father."

NLT

No one can take my life from me. I sacrifice it voluntarily. For I have the authority to lay it down when I want to and also to take it up again. For this is what my Father has commanded."

John 17:2
KJV

As thou hast given [G1325] him **power**[G1849] over all [G3956] flesh [G4561], that he should give [G1325] eternal [G166] life [G2222] to as many as thou hast given [G1325] him.

NKJV

as You have given Him authority over all flesh, that He should give eternal life to as many as

What Did Jesus Say About Authority?

You have given Him.

NLT

For you have given him authority over everyone.
He gives eternal life to each one you have given
him.

1 Corinthians 15:24
KJV

Then ^{G1534} cometh the end ^{G5056}, when ^{G3752} he
shall have delivered ^{G3860} up the kingdom ^{G932} to
God ^{G2316}, even ^{G2532} the Father ^{G3962}; when ^{G3752}
he shall have put ^{G2673} down ^{G2673} all ^{G3956} rule
^{G746} and all ^{G3956}**authority**^{G1849} and power ^{G1411}.

NKJV

Then *comes* the end, when He delivers the
kingdom to God the Father, when He puts an end
to all rule and all authority and power.

NLT

After that the end will come, when he will turn
the Kingdom over to God the Father, having
destroyed every ruler and authority and power.

Ephesians 1:21
KJV

Far ^{G5231} above ^{G5231} all ^{G3956} principality ^{G746},
and **power**^{G1849}, and might ^{G1411}, and dominion
^{G2963}, and every ^{G3956} name ^{G3686} that is named
^{G3687}, not only ^{G3440} in this ^{G3588} world ^{G165}, but
also ^{G2532} in that which is to come ^{G3195}:

NKJV

far above all principality and power and might
and dominion, and every name that is named, not
only in this age but also in that which is to come.

NLT

Now he is far above any ruler or authority or
power or leader or anything else—not only in
this world but also in the world to come.

Colossians 1:16
KJV

For by him were all [G3956] things created [G2936],
that are in heaven [G3772], and that are in earth
[G1093], visible [G3707] and invisible [G517], whether
[G1535] they be thrones [G2362], or [G1535] dominions
[G2963], or [G1535] principalities [G746], or [G1535]**powers
[G1849]:**all [G3956] things were created [G2936] by him,
and for him:

NKJV

For by Him all things were created that are in
heaven and that are on earth, visible and
invisible, whether thrones or dominions or
principalities or powers. All things were created
through Him and for Him.

NLT

for through him God created everything
in the heavenly realms and on earth.
He made the things we can see
and the things we can't see—
such as thrones, kingdoms, rulers, and authorities

in the unseen world.
Everything was created through him and for him.

Revelations 12:10
KJV

And I heard G191 a loud G3173 voice G5456 saying G3004 in heaven G3772, Now G737 is come G1096 salvation G4991, and strength G1411, and the kingdom G932 of our God G2316, and the **power**G1849of his Christ G5547: for the accuser G2725 of our brethren G80 is cast G2598 down G2598, which G3588 accused G2723 them before G1799 our God G2316 day G2250 and night G3571.

NKJV

Then I heard a loud voice saying in heaven, "Now salvation, and strength, and the kingdom of our God, and the power of His Christ have come, for the accuser of our brethren, who accused them before our God day and night, has been cast down.

NLT

Then I heard a loud voice shouting across the heavens,"It has come at last—salvation and powerand the Kingdom of our God,and the authority of his ChristFor the accuser of our brothers and sistershas been thrown down to earth—

the one who accuses thembefore our God day and night.

The power and authority of disciples

(5)

Matthew 10:1
KJV

> And when he had called [G4341] unto him his twelve [G1427] disciples [G3101], he gave [G1325] them **power** [G1849] against unclean [G169] spirits [G4151], to cast [G1544] them out, and to heal [G2323] all [G3956] manner of sickness [G3554] and all [G3956] manner of disease [G3119]

NKJV

> And when He had called His twelve disciples to *Him,* He gave them power *over* unclean spirits, to cast them out, and to heal all kinds of sickness and all kinds of disease.

NLT

> Jesus called his twelve disciples together and gave them authority to cast out evil spirits and to heal every kind of disease and illness.

Mark 3:15
KJV

> And to have [G2192] **power** [G1849] to heal [G2323] sicknesses [G3554], and to cast [G1544] out devils [G1140]:

NKJV

> and to have power to heal sicknesses and to cast out demons:

NLT

> giving them authority to cast out demons.

What Did Jesus Say About Authority?

Mark 6:7

KJV

> And he called ^{G4341} unto him the twelve ^{G1427}, and began ^{G756} to send ^{G649} them forth ^{G1614} by two ^{G1417} and two ^{G1417}; and gave ^{G1325} them **power** ^{G1849}over unclean ^{G169} spirits ^{G4151};

NKJV

> And He called the twelve to *Himself,* and began to send them out two *by* two, and gave them power over unclean spirits.

NLT

> And he called his twelve disciples together and began sending them out two by two, giving them authority to cast out evil spirits.

Luke 9:1

KJV

> Then ^{G1161} he called ^{G4779} his twelve ^{G1427} disciples ^{G3101} together ^{G4779}, and gave ^{G1325} them power ^{G1411} and **authority** ^{G1849}over ^{G1909} all ^{G3956} devils ^{G1140}, and to cure ^{G2323} diseases ^{G3554}

NKJV.

> Then He called His twelve disciples together and gave them power and authority over all demons, and to cure diseases.

NLT

> One day Jesus called together his twelve disciples and gave them power and authority to

cast out demons and to heal all diseases.

Luke 10:19
KJV
> Behold [G2400], I give [G1325] unto you **power** [G1849] to tread [G3961] on [G1883] serpents [G3789] and scorpions [G4651], and over [G1909] all [G3956] the power [G1411] of the enemy [G2190]: and nothing [G3762] shall by any [G3364] means [G3364] hurt [G91] you.

NKJV
> Behold, I give you the authority to trample on serpents and scorpions, and over all the power of the enemy, and nothing shall by any means hurt you.

NLT,
> Look, I have given you authority over all the power of the enemy, and you can walk among snakes and scorpions and crush them. Nothing will injure you.

The power, authority and rights of servants/believers (11)

John 1:12
KJV
> But as many [G3745] as received [G2983] him, to them gave [G1325] he **power** [G1849] to become [G1096] the sons [G5043] of God [G2316], even to them that believe [G4100] on [G1519] his name [G3686]:

NKJV

What Did Jesus Say About Authority?

But as many as received Him, to them He gave
the right to become children of God, to those
who believe in His name:

NLT

But to all who believed him and accepted him,
he gave the right to become children of God.

Mark 13:34
KJV

For the Son of man is as a man ^{G444} taking a far
journey ^{G590}, who left ^{G863} his house ^{G3614}, and
gave G1325 <u>**authority**</u> ^{G1849} to his servants ^{G1401},
and to every ^{G1538} man his work ^{G2041}, and
commanded ^{G1781} the porter ^{G2377} to watch ^{G1127}.

NKJV

It is like a man going to a far country, who left
his house and gave authority to his servants, and
to each his work, and commanded the
doorkeeper to watch.

NLT

"The coming of the Son of Man can be
illustrated by the story of a man going on a long
trip. When he left home, he gave each of his
slaves instructions about the work they were to
do, and he told the gatekeeper to watch for his
return.

Luke 19:17
KJV

And he said ^{G2036} unto him, Well ^{G2095}, thou good

G18 servant G1401: because G3754 thou hast been G1096 faithful G4103 in a very G1646 little G1646, have G2192 thou **authority** G1849 over G1883 ten G1176 cities G4172.

NKJV

And he said to him, 'Well *done,* good servant; because you were faithful in a very little, have authority over ten cities.'

NLT

"'Well done!' the king exclaimed. 'You are a good servant. You have been faithful with the little I entrusted to you, so you will be governor of ten cities as your reward.'

Acts 5:4

KJV

Whiles it remained G3306, was it not thine G4671 own? and after it was sold G4097, was it not in thine G3588_G4674 own **power** G1849? Why G5101 hast thou conceived G5087 this G5124 thing G4229 in thine G4675 heart G2588? thou hast not lied G5574 unto men G444, but unto God G2316.

NKJV

While it remained, was it not your own? And after it was sold, was it not in your own control? Why have you conceived this thing in your heart? You have not lied to men but to God."

NLT

The property was yours to sell or not sell, as you

wished. And after selling it, the money was also yours to give away. How could you do a thing like this? You weren't lying to us but to God!"

1 Corinthians 7:37
KJV

Nevertheless G1161 he that standeth G2476 stedfast G1476 in his heart G2588, having G2192 no G3361 necessity G318, but hath G2192**power G1849** over G4012 his own G2398 will G2307, and hath so G5124 decreed G2919 in his heart G2588 that he will keep G5083 his virgin G3933, doeth G4160 well G2573.

NKJV

Nevertheless he who stands steadfast in his heart, having no necessity, but has power over his own will, and has so determined in his heart that he will keep his virgin, does well.

NLT

But if he has decided firmly not to marry and there is no urgency and he can control his passion, he does well not to marry.

1 Corinthians 8:9
KJV

But take heed G991 lest G3381 by any G3381 means G4458 this G3778**liberty G1849** of yours G5216 become G1096 a stumbling block G4348 to them that are weak G770.

NKJV

But beware lest somehow this liberty of yours

become a stumbling block to those who are
weak.

NLT

But you must be careful so that your freedom
does not cause others with a weaker conscience
to stumble.

1 Corinthians 11:10

KJV

For this [G5124] cause [G1223] ought [G3784] the woman
[G1135] to have [G2192]**power** [G1849] on [G1909] her head
[G2776] because [G1223] of the angels [G32].

NKJV

For this reason the woman ought to have *a
symbol of* authority on *her* head, because of the
angels.

NLT

For this reason, and because the angels are
watching, a woman should wear a covering on
her head to show she is under authority.

Colossians 2:10

KJV

And ye are complete [G4137] in him, which [G3739] is
the head [G2776] of all [G3956] principality [G746] and
power [G1849]:

NKJV

and you are complete in Him, who is the head of
all principality and power.

NLT

So you also are complete through your union with Christ, who is the head over every ruler and authority.

Revelations 2:26

KJV

And he that overcometh G3528, and keepeth G5083 my works G2041 unto the end G5056, to him will I give G1325**power G1849** over G1909 the nations G1484:

NKJV

And he who overcomes, and keeps My works until the end, to him I will give power over the nations—

NLT

To all who are victorious, who obey me to the very end, To them I will give authority over all the nations.

Revelations 20:6

KJV

Blessed G3107 and holy G40 is he that hath G2192 part G3313 in the first G4413 resurrection G386: on G1909 such G5130 the second G1208 death G2288 hath G2192 no G3756**power G1849**, but they shall be priests G2409 of God G2316 and of Christ G5547, and shall reign G936 with him a thousand G5507 years G2094.

NKJV

Blessed and holy *is* he who has part in the first resurrection. Over such the second death has no power, but they shall be priests of God and of Christ, and shall reign with Him a thousand years.

NLT

Blessed and holy are those who share in the first resurrection. For them the second death holds no power, but they will be priests of God and of Christ and will reign with him a thousand years.

Revelations 22:14

KJV

Blessed G3107 are they that do G4160 his commandments G1785, that they may have G2071 **right** G1849 to the tree G3586 of life G2222, and may enter G1525 in through the gates G4440 into G1519 the city G4172.

NKJV

Blessed *are* those who do His commandments, that they may have the right to the tree of life, and may enter through the gates into the city.

NLT

Blessed are those who wash their robes. They will be permitted to enter through the gates of the city and eat the fruit from the tree of life.

The power, authority and rights of apostles (11)

Acts 8:19

KJV

Saying [G3004], Give [G1325] me also [G2504] this [G5026] **power** [G1849], that on [G2007] whomsoever [G3739_G302] I lay [G2007] hands [G5495], he may receive [G2983] the Holy [G40] Ghost [G4151].

NKJV

saying, "Give me this power also, that anyone on whom I lay hands may receive the Holy Spirit."

NLT

"Let me have this power, too," he exclaimed, "so that when I lay my hands on people, they will receive the Holy Spirit!"

1 Corinthians 9:4–6

KJV

Have [G2192] we not **power** [G1849] to eat [G5315] and to drink [G4095]? Have [G2192] we not **power** [G1849] to lead [G4013] about [G4013] a sister [G79], a wife [G1135], as well [G2532] as other [G3062] apostles [G652], and as the brethren [G80] of the Lord [G2962], and Cephas [G2786]?Or [G2228] I only [G3441] and Barnabas [G921], have [G2192] not we **power** [G1849] to forbear [G3361] working [G2038]?

NKJV

Do we have no right to eat and drink? Do we have no right to take along a believing wife, as *do* also the other apostles, the brothers of the Lord, and Cephas? Or *is it* only Barnabas and I *who* have no right to refrain from working?

NLT

Don't we have the right to live in your homes
and share your meals? Don't we have the right to
bring a Christian wife with us as the other
disciples and the Lord's brothers do, and as Peter
does? Or is it only Barnabas and I who have to
work to support ourselves?

1 Corinthians 9:12
KJV

If G1487 others G243 be partakers G3348 of this
G3588**power** G1849 over you, are not we rather
G3123? Nevertheless G235 we have G2192 not used
G5530 this G5026**power** G1849; but suffer G4722 all
G3956 things, lest G2443_G3361 we should hinder
G5100_G1464_G1325 the gospel G2098 of Christ G5547.

NKJV

If others are partakers of *this* right over you, *are*
we not even more? Nevertheless we have not
used this right, but endure all things lest we
hinder the gospel of Christ.

NLT

If you support others who preach to you,
shouldn't we have an even greater right to be
supported? But we have never used this right.
We would rather put up with anything than be an
obstacle to the Good News about Christ.

1 Corinthians 9:18
KJV

What [G5101] is my reward [G3408] then [G3767]? Verily that, when I preach [G2097] the gospel [G2097], I may make [G5087] the gospel [G2098] of Christ [G5547] without [G77] charge [G77], that I abuse [G2710] not my **power [G1849]** in the gospel [G2098].

NKJV

What is my reward then? That when I preach the gospel, I may present the gospel of Christ without charge, that I may not abuse my authority in the gospel.

NLT

What then is my pay? It is the opportunity to preach the Good News without charging anyone. That's why I never demand my rights when I preach the Good News.

2 Corinthians 10:8

KJV

For though [G1437] I should boast [G2744] somewhat [G5100] more [G4055] of our **authority [G1849]**, which [G3739] the Lord [G2962] hath given [G1325] us for edification [G3619], and not for your [G5216] destruction [G2506], I should not be ashamed [G153]:

NKJV

For even if I should boast somewhat more about our authority, which the Lord gave us for edification and not for your destruction, I shall not be ashamed—

NLT

I may seem to be boasting too much about the authority given to us by the Lord. But our authority builds you up; it doesn't tear you down. So I will not be ashamed of using my authority.

2 Corinthians 13:10

KJV

Therefore [G1223_G5124] I write [G1125] these [G5023] things being absent [G548], lest [G2443_G3361] being present [G3918] I should use [G5530] sharpness [G664], according [G2596] to the **power** [G1849] which [G3739] the Lord [G2962] hath given [G1325] me to edification [G3619], and not to destruction [G2506].

NKJV

Therefore I write these things being absent, lest being present I should use sharpness, according to the authority which the Lord has given me for edification and not for destruction.

NLT

I am writing this to you before I come, hoping that I won't need to deal severely with you when I do come. For I want to use the authority the Lord has given me to strengthen you, not to tear you down.

2 Thessalonians 3:9

KJV

Not because [G3754] we have [G2192] not **power** [G1849], but to make [G1325] ourselves [G1438] an ensample [G5179] unto you to follow [G3401] us.

NKJV

not because we do not have authority, but to make ourselves an example of how you should follow us.

NLT

We certainly had the right to ask you to feed us, but we wanted to give you an example to follow.

Hebrews 13:10
KJV

We have G2192 an altar G2379, whereof G1537_G3739 they have G2192 no G3756**right** G1849 to eat G5315 which serve G3000 the tabernacle G4633.

NKJV

We have an altar from which those who serve the tabernacle have no right to eat.

NLT

We have an altar from which the priests in the Tabernacle have no right to eat.

The power and authority of angels (2)

Revelations 14:18
KJV

And another G243 angel G32 came G1831 out from the altar G2379, which had G2192**power** G1849 over G1909 fire G4442; and cried G5455 with a loud G3173 cry G2906 to him that had G2192 the sharp G3691 sickle G1407, saying G3004, Thrust G3992 in thy sharp G3691 sickle G1407, and gather G5166 the clusters G1009 of the vine G288 of the earth G1093; for her grapes G4718 are fully ripe G187.

NKJV

And another angel came out from the altar, who had power over fire, and he cried with a loud cry to him who had the sharp sickle, saying, "Thrust in your sharp sickle and gather the clusters of the vine of the earth, for her grapes are fully ripe."

NLT

Then another angel, who had power to destroy with fire, came from the altar. He shouted to the angel with the sharp sickle, "Swing your sickle now to gather the clusters of grapes from the vines of the earth, for they are ripe for judgment."

Revelations 18:1

KJV

And after G3326 these G5023 things I saw G1492 another G243 angel G32 come G2597 down G2597 from heaven G3772, having G2192 great G3173**power G1849**; and the earth G1093 was lightened G5461 with his glory G1391.

NKJV

After these things I saw another angel coming down from heaven, having great authority, and the earth was illuminated with his glory.

NLT

> After all this I saw another angel come down from heaven with great authority, and the earth grew bright with his splendor.

The power of witnesses (2)

Revelations 11:6

KJV

> These [G3778] have [G2192]**power** [G1849] to shut [G2808] heaven [G3772], that it rain [G1026_G5205] not in the days [G2250] of their prophecy [G4394]: and have [G2192]**power** [G1849] over [G1909] waters [G5204] to turn [G4762] them to blood [G129], and to smite [G3960] the earth [G1093] with all [G3956] plagues [G4127], as often [G3740] as they will [G2309].

NKJV

> These have power to shut heaven, so that no rain falls in the days of their prophecy; and they have power over waters to turn them to blood, and to strike the earth with all plagues, as often as they desire.

NLT

> They have power to shut the sky so that no rain will fall for as long as they prophesy. And they have the power to turn the rivers and oceans into blood, and to strike the earth with every kind of plague as often as they wish.

Chapter 6

Authority, CivilandReligious Authorities

In the followings Scripture verses, Exousia G1849 identifies Civil, Religious Authorities.

The power and authority of governments, governor (10)

The power and jurisdiction of Herod and Pilate (3)

The authority of the centurion 2)

The questions the chief priests and elders had about Jesus' authority (11)

The authority Saul had from the chief priests and elders to imprison and kill all who call on the name (3)

The power and authority of Governments, governor (10)

Luke 12:11
KJV

And when G3752 they bring G4374 you unto the synagogues G4864, and unto magistrates G746, and **powers** G1849, take ye no G3361 thought G3309 how G4459 or G2228 what G5101 thing ye shall answer G626, or G2228 what G5101 ye shall say G2036:

NKJV

"Now when they bring you to the synagogues and magistrates and authorities, do not worry about how or what you should answer, or what you should say.

NLT

"And when you are brought to trial in the synagogues and before rulers and authorities, don't worry about how to defend yourself or what to say.

Luke 20:20
KJV

And they watched G3906 him, and sent G649 forth G649 spies G1455, which should feign G5271 themselves G1438 just G1342 men, that they might take G1949 hold G1949 of his words G3056, that so G1519 they might deliver G3860 him unto the power G746 and **authority** G1849 of the governor G2230.

NKJV

So they watched *Him,* and sent spies who pretended to be righteous, that they might seize on His words, in order to deliver Him to the power and the authority of the governor.

NLT

Watching for their opportunity, the leaders sent spies pretending to be honest men. They tried to get Jesus to say something that could be reported to the Roman governor so he would arrest Jesus.

Romans 13:1–3

KJV

Let every ^{G3956} soul ^{G5590} be subject ^{G5293} unto the higher ^{G5242}**powers** ^{G1849}. For there is no ^{G3756}**power** ^{G1849} but of God ^{G2316}: the **powers** ^{G1849} that be are ordained ^{G5021} of God ^{G2316}. Whosoever ^{G3588} therefore ^{G5620} resisteth ^{G498} the **power** ^{G1849}, resisteth ^{G436} the ordinance ^{G1296} of God ^{G2316}: and they that resist ^{G436} shall receive ^{G2983} to themselves ^{G1438} damnation ^{G2917}. For rulers ^{G758} are not a terror ^{G5401} to good ^{G18} works ^{G2041}, but to the evil ^{G2556}. Wilt ^{G2309} thou then ^{G1161} not be afraid ^{G5399} of the **power** ^{G1849}? Do ^{G4160} that which is good ^{G18}, and thou shalt have ^{G2192} praise ^{G1868} of the same ^{G846}:

NKJV

Let every soul be subject to the governing authorities. For there is no authority except from God, and the authorities that exist are appointed by God. Therefore whoever resists the authority resists the ordinance of God, and those who resist will bring judgment on themselves. For rulers are not a terror to good works, but to evil. Do you want to be unafraid of the authority? Do what is good, and you will have praise from the same.

NLT

Everyone must submit to governing authorities. For all authority comes from God, and those in positions of authority have been placed there by God. So anyone who rebels against authority is rebelling against what God has instituted, and they will be punished. For the authorities do not strike fear in people who are doing right, but in those who are doing wrong. Would you like to live without fear of the authorities? Do what is right, and they will honor you.

Ephesians 3:10
KJV

To the intent [G2443] that now [G3568] unto the principalities [G746] and **powers** [G1849] in heavenly [G2032] places might be known [G1107] by the church [G1577] the manifold [G4182] wisdom [G4678] of God [G2316],

NKJV

to the intent that now the manifold wisdom of God might be made known by the church to the principalities and powers in the heavenly *places,*

NLT

God's purpose in all this was to use the church to

display his wisdom in its rich variety to all the unseen rulers and authorities in the heavenly places.

Titus 3:1
KJV

> Put G5279 them in mind G5279 to be subject G5293 to principalities G746 and **powers G1849**, to obey G3980 magistrates G3980, to be ready G2092 to every G3956 good G18 work G2041,

NKJV

> Remind them to be subject to rulers and authorities, to obey, to be ready for every good work,

NLT

> Remind the believers to submit to the government and its officers. They should be obedient, always ready to do what is good.

1 Peter 3:22
KJV

> Who G3739 is gone G4198 into G1519 heaven G3772, and is on G1722 the right G1188 hand of God G2316; angels G32 and **authorities G1849** and powers G1411 being made G5293 subject G5293 unto him.

NKJV

> who has gone into heaven and is at the right hand of God, angels and authorities and powers having been made subject to Him.

NLT

> Now Christ has gone to heaven. He is seated in the place of honor next to God, and all the angels and authorities and powers accept his authority.

The power and jurisdiction of Herod and Pilate (3)

Luke 23:7

KJV

> And as soon as he knew G1921 that he belonged G1510 unto Herod's G2264**jurisdiction** G1849, he sent G375 him to Herod G2264, who himself G846 also G2532 was at G1722 Jerusalem G2414 at G1722 that time G2250.

NKJV

> And as soon as he knew that He belonged to Herod's jurisdiction, he sent Him to Herod, who was also in Jerusalem at that time.

NLT

> When they said that he was, Pilate sent him to Herod Antipas, because Galilee was under Herod's jurisdiction, and Herod happened to be in Jerusalem at the time.

John 19:10

KJV

> Then G3767 saith G3004 Pilate G4091 unto him, Speakest G2980 thou not unto me? Knowest G1492 thou not that I have G2192**power** G1849 to crucify G4717 thee, and have G2192**power** G1849 to release

G630 thee?

NKJV

Then Pilate said to Him, "Are You not speaking to me? Do You not know that I have power to crucify You, and power to release You?"

NLT

"Why don't you talk to me?" Pilate demanded. "Don't you realize that I have the power to release you or crucify you?"

The authority of the centurion (2)

Matthew 8:9
KJV

For I am G1510 a man G444 under G5259**<u>authority</u> G1849**, having G2192 soldiers G4757 under G5259 me: and I say G3004 to this G5129 man, Go G4198, and he goeth G4198; and to another G243, Come G2064, and he cometh G2064; and to my servant G1401, Do G4160 this G5124, and he doeth G4160 it.

NKJV

For I also am a man under authority, having soldiers under me. And I say to this *one,* 'Go,' and he goes; and to another, 'Come,' and he comes; and to my servant, 'Do this,' and he does *it.*"

NLT

I know this because I am under the authority of my superior officers, and I have authority over my soldiers. I only need to say, 'Go,' and they go, or 'Come,' and they come. And if I say to my slaves, 'Do this,' they do it."

Luke 7:8
KJV

For I also [G2532] am [G1510] a man [G444] set [G5021] under [G5259]**authority** [G1849], having [G2192] under [G5259] me soldiers [G4757], and I say [G3004] unto one [G5129], Go [G4198], and he goeth [G4198]; and to another [G243], Come [G2064], and he cometh [G2064]; and to my servant [G1401], Do [G4160] this [G5124], and he doeth [G4238] it.

NKJV

For I also am a man placed under authority, having soldiers under me. And I say to one, 'Go,' and he goes; and to another, 'Come,' and he comes; and to my servant, 'Do this,' and he does *it.*"

NLT

I know this because I am under the authority of my superior officers, and I have authority over my soldiers. I only need to say, 'Go,' and they go, or 'Come,' and they come. And if I say to my slaves, 'Do this,' they do it."

The questions the chief priests and elders had about Jesus' authority
(11)

What Did Jesus Say About Authority?

Matthew 21:23–24
KJV

And when he was come G2064 into G1519 the temple G2411, the chief G749 priests G749 and the elders G4245 of the people G2992 came G4334 unto him as he was teaching G1321, and said G3004, By what G4169**authority** G1849doest G4160 thou these G5023 things? and who G5101 gave G1325 thee this G5026**authority** G1849?

And Jesus G2424 answered G611 and said G2036 unto them, I also G2504 will ask G2065 you one G1520 thing G3056, which G3739 if G1437 ye tell G2036 me, I in like G2504 wise will tell G2046 you by what G4169**authority** G1849 I do G4160 these G5023 things.

NKJV

Now when He came into the temple, the chief priests and the elders of the people confronted Him as He was teaching, and said, "By what authority are You doing these things? And who gave You this authority?"

But Jesus answered and said to them, "I also will ask you one thing, which if you tell Me, I likewise will tell you by what authority I do these things:

NLT

When Jesus returned to the Temple and began teaching, the leading priests and elders came up to him. They demanded, "By what authority are you doing all these things? Who gave you the right?"

"I'll tell you by what authority I do these things

if you answer one question," Jesus replied.

Matthew 21:27
KJV

And they answered [G611] Jesus [G2424], and said [G2036], We cannot [G3756_G1492] tell [G1492]. And he said [G5346] unto them, Neither [G3761] tell [G3004] I you by what [G4169]**authority** [G1849]I do [G4160] these [G5023] things.

NKJV

So they answered Jesus and said, "We do not know."
And He said to them, "Neither will I tell you by what authority I do these things.

NLT

So they finally replied, "We don't know."
And Jesus responded, "Then I won't tell you by what authority I do these things.

Mark 11:28–29
KJV

And say [G3004] unto him, By what [G4169]**authority** [G1849]doest [G4160] thou these [G5023] things? and who [G5101] gave [G1325] thee this [G5026]**authority** [G1849] to do [G4160] these [G5023] things?
And Jesus [G2424] answered [G611] and said [G2036] unto them, I will also [G2504] ask [G1905] of you one [G1520] question [G3056], and answer [G611] me, and I will tell [G2046] you by what [G4169]**authority** [G1849] I do [G4160] these [G5023] things.

What Did Jesus Say About Authority?

NKJV

> And they said to Him, "By what authority are You doing these things? And who gave You this authority to do these things?"
> But Jesus answered and said to them, "I also will ask you one question; then answer Me, and I will tell you by what authority I do these things:

NLT

> They demanded, "By what authority are you doing all these things? Who gave you the right to do them?"
> "I'll tell you by what authority I do these things if you answer one question," Jesus replied.

Mark 11:33

KJV

> And they answered ^{G611} and said ^{G3004} unto Jesus ^{G2424}, We cannot $^{G3756\_G1492}$ tell ^{G1492}. And Jesus ^{G2424} answering ^{G611} saith ^{G3004} unto them, Neither ^{G3761} do ^{G4160} I tell ^{G3004} you by what ^{G4169}**authority** ^{G1849} I do these ^{G5023} things.

NKJV

> So they answered and said to Jesus, "We do not know."
> And Jesus answered and said to them, "Neither will I tell you by what authority I do these things."

NLT

> So they finally replied, "We don't know."
> And Jesus responded, "Then I won't tell you by

what authority I do these things."

Luke 20:2
KJV

And spake G2036 unto him, saying G3004, Tell G2036 us, by what G4169**authority** G1849doest G4160 thou these G5023 things? Or G2228 who G5101 is he that gave G1325 thee this G5026**authority** G1849?

NKJV

and spoke to Him, saying, "Tell us, by what authority are You doing these things? Or who is he who gave You this authority?"

NLT

They demanded, "By what authority are you doing all these things? Who gave you the right?"

Luke 20:8
KJV

And Jesus G2424 said G2036 unto them, Neither G3761 tell G3004 I you by what G4169**authority** G1849I do G4160 these G5023 things.

NKJV

And Jesus said to them, "Neither will I tell you by what authority I do these things."

NLT

And Jesus responded, "Then I won't tell you by what authority I do these things."

The authority Saul had from chief

priests and elders to kill all who call on the name (3)

Acts 9:14

KJV

And here [G5602] he hath [G2192] **authority** [G1849] from the chief [G749] priests [G749] to bind [G1210] all [G3956] that call [G1941] on thy name [G3686].

NKJV

And here he has authority from the chief priests to bind all who call on Your name."

NLT

And he is authorized by the leading priests to arrest everyone who calls upon your name."

Acts 26:10

KJV

Which [G3739] thing I also [G2532] did in Jerusalem [G2414]: and many [G4183] of the saints [G40] did [G4160] I shut [G2623] up in prison [G5438], having received [G2983] **authority** [G1849] from the chief [G749] priests [G749]; and when they were put [G337] to death [G337], I gave [G2702] my voice [G5586] against [G2702] them.

NKJV

This I also did in Jerusalem, and many of the saints I shut up in prison, having received authority from the chief priests; and when they were put to death, I cast my vote against *them.*

NLT

Indeed, I did just that in Jerusalem. Authorized by the leading priests, I caused many believers there to be sent to prison. And I cast my vote against them when they were condemned to death.

Acts 26:12

KJV

Whereupon G1722_G3739 as I went G4198 to Damascus G1154 with **authority** G1849 and commission G2011 from the chief G749 priests G749,

NKJV

"While thus occupied, as I journeyed to Damascus with authority and commission from the chief priests,

NLT

"One day I was on such a mission to Damascus, armed with the authority and commission of the leading priests.

Chapter 7

Authority,
The Dark Side

In the following Scripture verses, Exousia G1849 identifies

The power and authority of the devil, Satan, darkness, and the kingdom of darkness (7)

The power and authority of the Beast and the Dragon (7)

The power of the pale horse, locusts, scorpions, and serpents (5)

The power and authority of the devil, Satan, darkness and rulers of darkness (7)

Luke 4:6
KJV

And the devil G1228 said G2036 unto him, All G537 this G5026**power** G1849 will I give G1325 thee, and the glory G1391 of them: for that is delivered G3860 unto me; and to whomsoever G3739_G1437 I will G2309 I give G1325 it.

NKJV

And the devil said to Him, "All this authority I will give You, and their glory; for *this* has been delivered to me, and I give it to whomever I wish.

NLT

"I will give you the glory of these kingdoms and authority over them," the devil said, "because they are mine to give to anyone I please.

Luke 22:53
KJV

When I was daily G2596_G2250 with you in the temple G2411, ye stretched G1614 forth G1614 no G3756 hands G5495 against G1909 me: but this G3778 is your G5216 hour G5610, and the **power** G1849 of darkness G4655.

NKJV

When I was with you daily in the temple, you did not try to seize Me. But this is your hour, and the power of darkness."

NLT

Why didn't you arrest me in the Temple? I was there every day. But this is your moment, the time when the power of darkness reigns."

Acts 26:18

KJV

To open [G455] their eyes [G3788], and to turn [G1994] them from darkness [G4655] to light [G5457], and from the **power** [G1849] of Satan [G4567] unto God [G2316], that they may receive [G2983] forgiveness [G859] of sins [G266], and inheritance [G2819] among [G1722] them which are sanctified [G37] by faith [G4102] that is in me.

NKJV

to open their eyes, *in order* to turn *them* from darkness to light, and *from* the power of Satan to God, that they may receive forgiveness of sins and an inheritance among those who are sanctified by faith in Me.'

NLT

to open their eyes, so they may turn from darkness to light and from the power of Satan to God. Then they will receive forgiveness for their sins and be given a place among God's people, who are set apart by faith in me.'

Ephesians 2:2
KJV

Wherein [G1722_G3757] in time [G4218] past ye walked [G4043] according [G2596] to the course [G165] of this [G5127] world [G2889], according [G2596] to the prince [G758] of the **power** [G1849] of the air [G109], the spirit [G4151] that now [G3568] worketh [G1754] in the children [G5207] of disobedience [G543]:

NKJV

in which you once walked according to the course of this world, according to the prince of the power of the air, the spirit who now works in the sons of disobedience,

NLT

You used to live in sin, just like the rest of the world, obeying the devil—the commander of the powers in the unseen world. He is the spirit at work in the hearts of those who refuse to obey God.

Ephesians 6:12
KJV

For we wrestle [G2076_G3823] not against [G4314] flesh [G4561] and blood [G129], but against [G4314] principalities [G746], against [G4314] **powers** [G1849], against [G4314] the rulers [G2888] of the darkness [G4655] of this [G5127] world [G165], against [G4314] spiritual [G4152] wickedness [G4189] in high [G2032] places.

NKJV

For we do not wrestle against flesh and blood,

but against principalities, against powers, against
the rulers of the darkness of this age, against
spiritual *hosts* of wickedness in the heavenly
places.

NLT

For we are not fighting against flesh-and-blood
enemies, but against evil rulers and authorities of
the unseen world, against mighty powers in this
dark world, and against evil spirits in the
heavenly places.

Colossians 1:13

KJV

Who [G3739] hath delivered [G4506] us from the **power**
[G1849]of darkness [G4655], and hath translated [G3179] us
into [G1519] the kingdom [G932] of his dear [G26] Son
[G5207].

NKJV

He has delivered us from the power of darkness
and conveyed *us* into the kingdom of the Son of
His love,

NLT

For he has rescued us from the kingdom of
darkness and transferred us into the Kingdom of
his dear Son,

Colossians 2:15

KJV

And having spoiled [G554] principalities [G746] and
powers [G1849], he made [G1165] a show [G1165] of them

openly [G1722_G3954], triumphing [G2358] over them in it.

NKJV

Having disarmed principalities and powers, He made a public spectacle of them, triumphing over them in it.

NLT

In this way, he disarmed the spiritual rulers and authorities. He shamed them publicly by his victory over them on the cross.

The power and authority of the Beast and Dragon (7)

Revelations 13:2

And the beast [G2342] which [G3739] I saw [G1492] was like [G3664] unto a leopard [G3917], and his feet [G4228] were as the feet [G4228] of a bear [G715], and his mouth [G4750] as the mouth [G4750] of a lion [G3023]: and the dragon [G1404] gave [G1325] him his power [G1411], and his seat [G2362], and great [G3173]**authority** [G1849].

NKJV

Now the beast which I saw was like a leopard, his feet were like *the feet of* a bear, and his mouth like the mouth of a lion. The dragon gave him his power, his throne, and great authority.

NLT

This beast looked like a leopard, but it had the feet of a bear and the mouth of a lion! And the dragon gave the beast his own power and throne and great authority.

Revelations 13:4–5

KJV

And they worshipped G4352 the dragon G1404 which G3739 gave G1325**power** G1849unto the beast G2342: and they worshipped G4352 the beast G2342, saying G3004, Who G5101 is like G3664 unto the beast G2342? Who G5101 is able G1410 to make G4170 war G4170 with him?

And there was given G1325 unto him a mouth G4750 speaking G2980 great G3173 things and blasphemies G988; and **power** G1849was given G1325 unto him to continue G4160 forty G5062 and two G1417 months G3376.

NKJV

So they worshiped the dragon who gave authority to the beast; and they worshiped the beast, saying, "Who *is* like the beast? Who is able to make war with him?"

And he was given a mouth speaking great things and blasphemies, and he was given authority to continue for forty-two months.

NLT

They worshiped the dragon for giving the beast such power, and they also worshiped the beast. "Who is as great as the beast?" they exclaimed. "Who is able to fight against him?"

Then the beast was allowed to speak great blasphemies against God. And he was given authority to do whatever he wanted for forty-two months.

Revelations 13:7
KJV

And it was given G1325 unto him to make G4160 war G4171 with the saints G40, and to overcome G3528 them: and **power G1849** was given G1325 him over G1909 all G3956 kindreds G5443, and tongues G1100, and nations G1484.

NKJV

It was granted to him to make war with the saints and to overcome them. And authority was given him over every tribe, tongue, and nation.

NLT

And the beast was allowed to wage war against God's holy people and to conquer them. And he was given authority to rule over every tribe and people and language and nation.

Revelations 13:12
KJV

And he exerciseth [G4160] all G3956 the**power [G1849]**of the first [G4413] beast [G2342] before [G1799] him, and causeth [G4160] the earth [G1093] and them which dwell [G2730] therein [G1722_G846] to worship [G4352] the first [G4413] beast [G2342], whose [G3739] deadly [G2288] wound [G4127] was healed [G2323].

NKJV

And he exercises all the authority of the first beast in his presence, and causes the earth and those who dwell in it to worship the first beast, whose deadly wound was healed.

NLT

He exercised all the authority of the first beast. And he required all the earth and its people to worship the first beast, whose fatal wound had been healed.

Revelations 17:12–13
KJV

And the ten [G1176] horns [G2768] which [G3739] thou sawest [G1492] are ten [G1176] kings [G935], which [G3748] have received [G2983] no [G3768] kingdom [G932] as yet [G3768]; but receive [G2983] **power** [G1849] as kings [G935] one [G3391] hour [G5610] with the beast [G2342].
These [G3778] have [G2192] one [G3391] mind [G1106], and shall give [G1239] their power [G1411] and **strength** [G1849] unto the beast [G2342].

NKJV

"The ten horns which you saw are ten kings who have received no kingdom as yet, but they receive authority for one hour as kings with the beast. These are of one mind, and they will give their power and authority to the beast.

NLT

The ten horns of the beast are ten kings who have not yet risen to power. They will be appointed to their kingdoms for one brief moment to reign with the beast. They will all agree to give him their power and authority.

The power of the pale horse, locusts, scorpions, and serpents (5)

Revelations 6:8

KJV

And I looked ^{G1492}, and behold ^{G2400} a pale ^{G5515} horse ^{G2462}: and his name ^{G3686} that sat ^{G2521} on ^{G1883} him was Death ^{G2288}, and Hell ^{G86} followed ^{G190} with him. And **power** ^{G1849} was given ^{G1325} unto them over ^{G1909} the fourth ^{G5067} part of the earth ^{G1093}, to kill ^{G615} with sword ^{G4501}, and with hunger ^{G3042}, and with death ^{G2288}, and with the beasts ^{G2342} of the earth ^{G1093}.

NKJV

So I looked, and behold, a pale horse. And the name of him who sat on it was Death, and Hades followed with him. And power was given to them over a fourth of the earth, to kill with sword, with hunger, with death, and by the beasts of the earth.

NLT

I looked up and saw a horse whose color was pale green. Its rider was named Death, and his companion was the Grave. These two were given authority over one-fourth of the earth, to kill with the sword and famine and disease and wild animals.

Revelation 9:3

KJV

And there came [G1831] out of the smoke [G2586] locusts [G200] upon the earth [G1093]: and unto them was given [G1325]**power** [G1849], as the scorpions [G4651] of the earth [G1093] have [G2192]**power** [G1849].

NKJV

Then out of the smoke locusts came upon the earth. And to them was given power, as the scorpions of the earth have power.

NLT

Then locusts came from the smoke and descended on the earth, and they were given power to sting like scorpions.

Revelations 9:10

KJV

And they had [G2192] tails [G3769] like [G3664] unto scorpions [G4651], and there were stings [G2759] in their tails [G3769]: and their **power** [G1849] was to hurt [G91] men [G444] five [G4002] months [G3376]

NKJV

They had tails like scorpions, and there were stings in their tails. Their power *was* to hurt men five months.

NLT

They had tails that stung like scorpions, and for

five months they had the power to torment people.

Revelations 9:19

KJV

For their **power** [G1849] is in their mouth [G4750], and in their tails [G3769]: for their tails [G3769] were like [G3664] unto serpents [G3789], and had [G2192] heads [G2776], and with them they do hurt [G91].

NKJV

For their power is in their mouth and in their tails; for their tails *are* like serpents, having heads; and with them they do harm.

NLT

Their power was in their mouths and in their tails. For their tails had heads like snakes, with the power to injure people.

Chapter 8

Six Remaining Words Sometimes Translated as Authority

Katexousiazo

Listed under rulers of this world

Exousiazo

Listed under rulers of this world

Dunastes

From
G1413
dunastes
Pronunciation: *doo-nas'-tace*
From G1410*Strong's Hebrew and Greek Dictionary*: a *ruler* or *officer:*—of great authority, mighty, potentate.

What Did Jesus Say About Authority?

From *Thayer'sGreek Dictionary*:
1) a prince, a potentate
2) a courtier, high officer, royal minister of great authority

Part of Speech: noun masculine

Total KJV Occurrences: 3

Translated as follows:
authority, 1
Acts 8:27
mighty, 1
Luke 1:52
potentate, 1
1 Tim. 6:15

Luke 1:52
KJV

He hath put ^{G2507} down ^{G2507}**the mighty** ^{G1413} from their seats ^{G2362}, and exalted ^{G5312} them of low ^{G5011} degree ^{G5011}.

NKJV

He has put down the mighty from *their* thrones, And exalted *the* lowly.

NLT

He has brought down princes from their thrones and exalted the humble.

Acts 8:27
KJV

And he arose [G450] and went [G4198]: and, behold [G2400], a man [G435] of Ethiopia [G128], an eunuch [G2135]**of great authority** [G1413]under Candace [G2582] queen [G938] of the Ethiopians [G128], who [G3739] had the charge [G1909] of all [G3956] her treasure [G1047], and had come [G2064] to Jerusalem [G2419] for to worship [G4352],

NKJV

So he arose and went. And behold, a man of Ethiopia, a eunuch of great authority under Candace the queen of the Ethiopians, who had charge of all her treasury, and had come to Jerusalem to worship,

NLT

So he started out, and he met the treasurer of Ethiopia, a eunuch of great authority under the Kandake, the queen of Ethiopia. The eunuch had gone to Jerusalem to worship,

1 Timothy 6:15
KJV

Which [G3739] in his times [G5550] he shall show [G1166], who [G3588] is the blessed [G3107] and only [G3441]**Potentate** [G1413], the King [G935] of kings [G936], and Lord [G2962] of lords [G2961];

NKJV

which He will manifest in His own time, *He who is* the blessed and only Potentate, the King of kings and Lord of lords,

NLT

> For at just the right time Christ will be revealed from heaven by the blessed and only almighty God, the King of all kings and Lord of all lords.

Huperoche

G5247
huperoche
Pronunciation: *hoop-er-okh-ay'*
From G5242*Strong's Hebrew and Greek Dictionary*:*prominence*, that is, (figuratively) *superiority* (in rank or character):—authority, excellency

From *Thayer's Greek Dictionary*:
1) elevation, pre-eminence, superiority
2) metaphorically excellence

Part of Speech: noun feminine

Total KJV Occurrences: 2

Translated as follows:
authority, 1
1 Tim. 2:2
excellency, 1
1 Cor. 2:1

1 Corinthians 2:1
KJV

> And I, brethren G80, when I came G2064 to you, came G2064 not with **excellency** G5247of speech

G3056 or G2228 of wisdom G4678, declaring G2605 unto you the testimony G3142 of God G2316.

NKJV

And I, brethren, when I came to you, did not come with excellence of speech or of wisdom declaring to you the testimony of God.

NLT

When I first came to you, dear brothers and sisters, I didn't use lofty words and impressive wisdom to tell you God's secret plan.

1 Timothy 2:2
KJV

For kings G935, and for all G3956 that are in **authority** G5247; that we may lead G1236 a quiet G2263 and peaceable G2272 life G979 in all G3956 godliness G2150 and honesty G4587.

NKJV

for kings and all who are in authority, that we may lead a quiet and peaceable life in all godliness and reverence.

NLT

Pray this way for kings and all who are in authority so that we can live peaceful and quiet lives marked by godliness and dignity.

Authenteo

G831
authenteo
Pronunciation: *ow-then-teh'-o*
From a compound of G846 *Strong's Hebrew and Greek Dictionary* and ἐντῃϛhentes (obsolete; a *worker*); to *actofoneself*, that is, (figuratively) *dominate:*—usurp authority over.

From *Thayer's Greek Dictionary*:
1) one who with his own hands kills another or himself
2) one who acts on his own authority, autocratic
3) an absolute master
4) to govern, exercise dominion over one

Part of Speech: verb

Total KJV Occurrences: 2

Translated as follows:
authority, 1
1 Tim. 2:12
usurp, 1
1 Tim. 2:12

1 Timothy 2:12
KJV

> But I suffer G2010 not a woman G1135 to teach G1321, nor G3761 to **usurp** [G831]**authority** [G831]over the man G435, but to be in silence G2271.

NKJV

And I do not permit a woman to teach or to have authority over a man, but to be in silence.

NLT
I do not let women teach men or have authority over them. Let them listen quietly.

Epitage

G2003
epitage
Pronunciation: *ep-ee-tag-ay'*
From G2004*Strong's Hebrew and Greek Dictionary*: an *injunction* or *decree*; by implication *authoritativeness:*—authority, commandment.

From *Thayer's Greek Dictionary*:
1) an injunction, mandate, command

Part of Speech: noun feminine

Total KJV Occurrences: 7

Translated as follows:
commandment, 6
Rom. 16:26; 1 Cor. 7:6; 1 Cor. 7:25; 2 Cor. 8:8; 1 Tim. 1:1; Titus 1:3
authority, 1
Titus 2:15

Romans 16:26
KJV

But now G3568 is made G5319 manifest G5319, and by the scriptures G1124 of the prophets G4397, according G2596 to the **commandment** G2003 of the everlasting G166 God G2316, made G1107 known G1107 to all G3956 nations G1484 for the obedience G5218 of faith G4102:

NKJV

but now made manifest, and by the prophetic Scriptures made known to all nations, according to the commandment of the everlasting God, for obedience to the faith—

NLT

But now as the prophets foretold and as the eternal God has commanded, this message is made known to all Gentiles everywhere, so that they too might believe and obey him.

1 Corinthians 7:6
KJV

But I speak G3004 this G5124 by permission G4774, and not of **commandment** G2003.

NKJV

But I say this as a concession, not as a commandment.

NLT

I say this as a concession, not as a command.

1 Corinthians 7:25

Now G1161 concerning G4012 virgins G3933 I have

G2192 no G3756**commandment** G2003 of the Lord
G2962: yet G1161 I give G1325 my judgment G1106, as
one that hath obtained G1653 mercy G1653 of the
Lord G2962 to be faithful G4103.

NKJV

Now concerning virgins: I have no
commandment from the Lord; yet I give
judgment as one whom the Lord in His mercy
has made trustworthy.

NLT

Now regarding your question about the young
women who are not yet married. I do not have a
command from the Lord for them. But the Lord
in his mercy has given me wisdom that can be
trusted, and I will share it with you.

2 Corinthians 8:8
KJV

I speak G3004 not by **commandment** G2003, but by
occasion G1223 of the forwardness G4710 of others
G2087, and to prove G1381 the sincerity G1103 of your
G5212 love G26.

NKJV

I speak not by commandment, but I am testing
the sincerity of your love by the diligence of
others.

NLT

I am not commanding you to do this. But I am
testing how genuine your love is by comparing it

with the eagerness of the other churches.

1 Timothy 1:1
KJV

Paul G3972, an apostle G652 of Jesus G2424 Christ G5547 by the **commandment** G2003of God G2316 our Saviour G4990, and Lord G2962 Jesus G2424 Christ G5547, which G3588 is our hope G1680;

NKJV

Paul, an apostle of Jesus Christ, by the commandment of God our Savior and the Lord Jesus Christ, our hope,

NLT

This letter is from Paul, an apostle of Christ Jesus, appointed by the command of God our Savior and Christ Jesus, who gives us hope.

Titus 1:3
KJV

But hath in due G2398 times G5550 manifested G5319 his word G3056 through G1722 preaching G2782, which G3739 is committed G4100 unto me according G2596 to the **commandment** G2003of God G2316 our Saviour G4990;

NKJV

but has in due time manifested His word through preaching, which was committed to me according to the commandment of God our Savior;

NLT

And now at just the right time he has revealed this message, which we announce to everyone. It is by the command of God our Savior that I have been entrusted with this work for him.

Titus 2:15

KJV

These [G5023] things speak [G2980], and exhort [G3870], and rebuke [G1651] with all [G3956]**authority** [G2003]. Let no [G3367] man [G3367] despise [G4065] thee.

NKJV

Speak these things, exhort, and rebuke with all authority. Let no one despise you.

NLT

You must teach these things and encourage the believers to do them. You have the authority to correct them when necessary, so don't let anyone disregard what you say.

Chapter 9

Authority,
Five Additional
Words in the
New King James Version
Sometimes Translated as
Authority

Emautou, Emauto, Emauton

From *Strong's Hebrew and Greek Dictionary*:
G1683
Emautou, emauto, emauton
Pronunciation: *em-ow-too', em-ow-to', em-ow-ton*
Genitive, dative and accusative of a compound of
G1700 and G846; *ofmyself:*—me, mine own (self),
myself.

From *Thayer's Greek Dicationary*:
1) I, me, myself, etc.

Part of Speech: pronoun

What Did Jesus Say About Authority?

Total KJV Occurrences: 37

Translated as follows:
myself, 30
Luke 7:7; John 5:31; John 7:17; John 7:28; John 8:14; John 8:18; John 8:28; John 8:42; John 8:54; John 10:18; John 12:49; John 14:3; John 14:10; John 14:21; John 17:19; Acts 20:24; Acts 24:10; Acts 26:2; Acts 26:9; Rom. 11:4; 1 Cor. 4:4; 1 Cor. 7:6–7 (2); 1 Cor. 9:19; 2 Cor. 2:1; 2 Cor. 11:7; 2 Cor. 11:9 (2); 2 Cor. 12:5; Gal. 2:18
mine, 3
John 5:30; 1 Cor. 4:3; 1 Cor. 10:33
own, 2
1 Cor. 4:3; 1 Cor. 10:33
self, 2
John 5:30; 1 Cor. 4:3

John 17:17
KJV

> If [G1437] any [G5100] man will [G2309] do [G4160] his will [G2307], he shall know [G1097] of the doctrine [G1322], whether [G4220] it be of God [G2316], or [G2228] whether I speak [G2980]**of myself** [G1683].

NKJV

> If anyone wills to do His will, he shall know concerning the doctrine, whether it is from God or *whether* I speak on **My own *authority*.**

NLT

> Anyone who wants to do the will of God will know whether my teaching is from God or is

merely my own.

John 12:49
KJV

> For I have G2192 not spoken G2980**of myself G1683**; but the Father G3962 which G3588 sent G3992 me, he gave G1325 me a commandment G1785, what G5101 I should say G2036, and what G5101 I should speak G2980.

NKJV

> For I have not spoken on **My own *authority***; but the Father who sent Me gave Me a command, what I should say and what I should speak.

NLT

> I don't speak on my own authority. The Father who sent me has commanded me what to say and how to say it.

John 14:10
KJV

> Believest G4100 thou not that I am in the Father G3962, and the Father G3962 in me? the words G4487 that I speak G2980 unto you I speak G2980**not of myself G1683**: but the Father G3962 that dwelleth G3306 in me, he doeth G4160 the works G2041.

NKJV

> Do you not believe that I am in the Father, and the Father in Me? The words that I speak to you I do not speak on **My own *authority;***but the Father who dwells in Me does the works.

NLT

Don't you believe that I am in the Father and the Father is in me? The words I speak are not my own, but my Father who lives in me does his work through me.

Heautou

From *Strong's Hebrew and Greek Dictionary*:
G1438
heautou
Pronunciation: *heh-ow-too'*
(Including all the other cases); from a reflexive pronoun otherwise obsolete and the genitive (dative or accusative) of G846; *him* (*her*, *it*, *them*, also [in conjunction with the personal pronoun of the other persons] *my*, *thy*, *our*, *your*) -self (-selves), etc.:— alone, her (own, -self), (he) himself, his (own), itself, one (to) another, our (thine) own (-selves), + that she had, their (own, own selves), (of) them (-selves), they, thyself, you, your (own, own conceits, own selves, -selves).

From *Thayer's Greek Dictionary*:
1) himself, herself, itself, themselves
Part of Speech: pronoun

Total KJV Occurrences: 301

Translated as follows:
himself, 114
Matt. 12:26; Matt. 12:45 (2); Matt. 13:21; Matt.

16:24; Matt. 18:4; Matt. 23:12 (2); Matt. 27:42; Mark 3:26; Mark 5:5; Mark 5:30; Mark 8:34; Mark 12:33; Mark 15:31; Luke 7:39; Luke 9:23; Luke 9:25; Luke 10:29; Luke 11:18; Luke 11:26; Luke 12:17; Luke 12:21; Luke 14:11 (2); Luke 15:15; Luke 15:17; Luke 18:3–4 (2); Luke 18:11; Luke 18:14 (2); Luke 19:12; Luke 23:2; Luke 23:35; Luke 24:12; Luke 24:27; John 2:24; John 5:18–19 (2); John 5:26 (2); John 6:61; John 7:18; John 8:22; John 11:38; John 11:51; John 13:4; John 13:32; John 16:13; John 19:7; John 21:1; John 21:7; Acts 1:3; Acts 5:36; Acts 8:9; Acts 8:34; Acts 10:17; Acts 12:11; Acts 14:17; Acts 16:27; Acts 19:31; Acts 25:4; Acts 28:16; Rom. 14:7 (2); Rom. 14:12; Rom. 14:22; Rom. 15:3; 1 Cor. 3:18; 1 Cor. 11:28–29 (2); 1 Cor. 14:4; 1 Cor. 14:28; 2 Cor. 5:18–19 (2); 2 Cor. 10:7 (2); 2 Cor. 10:18; Gal. 1:4; Gal. 2:12; Gal. 2:20; Gal.6:3–4 (2); Eph. 2:15; Eph. 5:2; Eph. 5:25; Eph. 5:27–28 (2); Eph. 5:33; Phil. 2:7–8 (2); Phil. 3:21; 2 Thess. 2:4 (2); 1 Tim. 2:6; 2 Tim. 2:13; 2 Tim. 2:21; Titus 2:14 (2); Heb. 5:3–5 (4); Heb. 6:13; Heb. 7:27; Heb. 9:7; Heb. 9:14; Heb. 9:25; James 1:24; James 1:27; 1 John 3:3; 1 John 5:18

themselves, 57

Matt. 9:3; Matt. 14:15; Matt. 16:7; Matt. 19:12; Matt. 21:25; Matt. 21:38; Mark 2:8; Mark 4:17; Mark 6:36; Mark 6:51; Mark 9:8; Mark 9:10; Mark 10:26; Mark 11:31; Mark 12:7; Mark 14:4; Mark 16:3; Luke 7:30; Luke 7:49; Luke 18:9; Luke 20:5; Luke 20:14; Luke 20:20; Luke 22:23; Luke 23:12; John 7:35; John 11:55; John 12:19; Acts 23:12; Acts 23:21; Acts 28:29; Rom. 1:24; Rom. 1:27;

Rom. 2:14; Rom. 13:2; 1 Cor. 16:15; 2 Cor. 5:15; 2
Cor. 10:12 (5); Eph. 4:19; Phil. 2:3; 1 Tim. 2:9; 1
Tim. 3:13; 1 Tim. 6:10; 1 Tim. 6:19; 2 Tim. 4:3;
Heb. 6:6; 1 Pet. 1:12; 1 Pet. 3:5; 2 Pet. 2:1; Jude
1:12; Jude 1:19; Rev. 6:15; Rev. 8:6

yourselves, 37

Matt. 3:9; Matt. 16:8; Matt. 23:31; Matt. 25:9; Mark
9:33; Mark 9:50; Mark 13:9; Luke 3:8; Luke 12:33;
Luke 12:57; Luke 16:9; Luke 16:15; Luke 17:3;
Luke 17:14; Luke 21:34; Luke 22:17; Luke 23:28;
Acts 5:35; Acts 13:46; Acts 15:29; Acts 20:28;
Rom. 6:11; Rom. 6:13; Rom. 6:16; Rom. 12:19; 2
Cor. 7:11; 2 Cor. 13:5; Eph. 5:19; 1 Thess. 5:13; 1
Thess. 5:15; Heb. 10:34; James 2:4; 1 Pet. 4:8; 1
John 5:21; 2 John 1:8; Jude 1:20–21 (2)

own, 24

Luke 14:26; Luke 22:71; John 20:10; Acts 7:21;
Rom. 4:19; Rom. 8:3; Rom. 11:25; Rom. 12:16;
Rom. 16:4; Rom. 16:18; 1 Cor. 6:19; 1 Cor. 7:2; 1
Cor. 10:24; 1 Cor. 10:29; 1 Cor. 13:5; Gal. 6:4;
Eph. 5:28–29 (2); Phil. 2:4; Phil. 2:12; 1 Thess. 2:8;
2 Thess. 3:12; Jude 1:13; Jude 1:18

ourselves, 21

Acts 23:14; Rom. 8:23; Rom. 15:1; 1 Cor. 11:31; 2
Cor. 1:9 (2); 2 Cor. 3:1; 2 Cor. 3:5 (2); 2 Cor. 4:2; 2
Cor. 4:5 (2); 2 Cor. 5:12; 2 Cor. 6:4; 2 Cor. 7:1; 2
Cor. 10:12 (2); 2 Cor. 10:14; 2 Thess. 3:9; Heb.
10:25; 1 John 1:8

itself, 9

Matt. 6:34; Matt. 12:25 (2); Mark 3:24–25 (2); Luke
11:17; John 15:4; Rom. 14:14; Eph. 4:16

your, 8

Luke 21:30; Rom. 11:25; 1 Cor. 6:19; 2 Cor. 13:5

(2); Eph. 5:25; Phil. 2:12; James 1:22
another, 7
Mark 9:10; 1 Cor. 6:7; Eph. 4:32; Col. 3:13; Col.
3:16; Heb. 3:13; 1 Pet. 4:10
one, 6
1 Cor. 6:7; Eph. 4:32; Col. 3:13; Col. 3:16; Heb.
3:13; 1 Pet. 4:10
herself, 5
Matt. 9:21; Luke 1:24; Rev. 2:20; Rev. 19:7 (2)
selves, 4
Luke 21:30; 2 Cor. 13:5 (3)
thyself, 3
John 18:34; Rom. 13:9; Gal. 5:14
conceits, 2
Rom. 11:25; Rom. 12:16
alone, 1
James 2:16–17 (2)
home, 1
John 20:10
thine, 1
1 Cor. 10:29
troubled, 1
John 11:33

John 11:51
KJV

And this ^{G5124} spake ^{G2036} he **not of himself** ^{G1438}:
but being ^{G5607} high ^{G749} priest ^{G749} that year
^{G1763}, he prophesied ^{G4395} that Jesus ^{G2424} should
^{G3195} die ^{G599} for that nation ^{G1484};

NKJV

Now this he did not say on **his own**

authority; but being high priest that year he prophesied that Jesus would die for the nation,

NLT

He did not say this on his own; as high priest at that time he was led to prophesy that Jesus would die for the entire nation.

John 16:13

KJV

Howbeit when G3752 he, the Spirit G4151 of truth G225, is come G2064, he will guide G3594 you into G1519 all G3956 truth G225: for he shall not speak G2980 of **himself** G1438; but whatsoever G3745_G302 he shall hear G191, that shall he speak G2980: and he will show G312 you things to come G2064.

NKJV

However, when He, the Spirit of truth, has come, He will guide you into all truth; for He will not speak on **His own *authority***, but whatever He hears He will speak; and He will tell you things to come.

NLT

When the Spirit of truth comes, he will guide you into all truth. He will not speak on his own but will tell you what he has heard. He will tell you about the future.

Archon

From *Strong's Hebrew and Greek Dictionary*:

What Did Jesus Say About Authority?

G758
archon
Pronunciation: *ar'-khone*
Present participle of G757; a *first* (in rank or power):—chief (ruler), magistrate, prince, ruler.

From *Thayer's Greek Dictionary*:
1) a ruler, commander, chief, leader

Part of Speech: noun masculine

Total KJV Occurrences: 38

Translated as follows:
rulers, 14
Luke 23:13; Luke 23:35; Luke 24:20; John 7:26; John 7:48; John 12:42; Acts 3:17; Acts 4:5; Acts 4:8; Acts 13:26–27 (2); Acts 14:5; Acts 16:19; Rom. 13:3
prince, 8
Matt. 9:34; Matt. 12:24; Mark 3:22; John 12:31; John 14:30; John 16:11; Eph. 2:2; Rev. 1:5
ruler, 8
Matt. 9:18; Luke 8:41; Luke 18:18; John 3:1; Acts 7:27; Acts 7:35 (2); Acts 23:5
chief, 3
Luke 11:15; Luke 14:1; John 12:42
princes, 3
Matt. 20:25; 1 Cor. 2:6; 1 Cor. 2:8
magistrate, 1
Luke 12:58
ruler's, 1
Matt. 9:23

Acts 16:19
KJV

And when her masters [G2962] saw [G1492] that the hope [G1680] of their gains [G2039] was gone [G1831], they caught [G1949] Paul [G3972] and Silas [G4609], and drew [G1670] them into [G1519] the marketplace [G58]**unto the rulers** [G758],

NKJV

But when her masters saw that their hope of profit was gone, they seized Paul and Silas and dragged *them* into the marketplace **to the authorities.**

NLT

Her masters' hopes of wealth were now shattered, so they grabbed Paul and Silas and dragged them before the authorities at the marketplace.

Dunatos

From *Strong's Hebrew and Greek Dictionary*:
G1415
dunatos
Pronunciation: *doo-nat-os'*
From G1410; *powerful* or *capable* (literally or figuratively); neuter *possible:*—able, could, (that is) mighty (man), possible, power, strong.

From *Thayer's Greek Dictionary*:

What Did Jesus Say About Authority?

1) able, powerful, mighty, strong
1a) mighty in wealth and influence
1b) strong in soul
1b1) to bear calamities and trials with fortitude and patience
1b2) strong in Christian virtue
2) to be able (to do something)
2a) mighty, excelling in something
2b) having power for something

Part of Speech: adjective

Total KJV Occurrences: 35

Translated as follows:
possible, 13
Matt. 19:26; Matt. 24:24; Matt. 26:39; Mark 9:23; Mark 10:27; Mark 13:22; Mark 14:35–36 (2); Luke 18:27; Acts 2:24; Acts 20:16; Rom. 12:18; Gal. 4:15
able, 10
Luke 14:31; Acts 25:5; Rom. 4:21; Rom. 11:23; Rom. 14:4; 2 Cor. 9:8; 2 Tim. 1:12; Titus 1:9; Heb. 11:19; James 3:2
mighty, 7
Luke 1:49; Luke 24:19; Acts 7:22; Acts 18:24; 1 Cor. 1:26; 2 Cor. 10:4; Rev. 6:15
strong, 3
Rom. 15:1; 2 Cor. 12:10; 2 Cor. 13:9
could, 1
Acts 11:17
power, 1
Rom. 9:22

Acts 25:5
KJV

> Let them therefore [G3767], said [G5346] he, which among [G1722]**you are able** [G1415], go [G4782] down [G4782] with me, and accuse [G2723] this [G846] man [G435], if [G1487] there be any [G1536] wickedness [G824] in him.

NKJV

> "Therefore," he said, "let those **who have authority** among you go down with *me* and accuse this man, to see if there is any fault in him."

NLT

> So he said, "Those of you in authority can return with me. If Paul has done anything wrong, you can make your accusations."

Kuriotes

From *Strong's Hebrew and Greek Dictionary*:
G2963
kuriotes
Pronunciation: *koo-ree-ot'-ace*
From G2962; *mastery*, that is, (concretely and collectively) *rulers:*—dominion, government.

From *Thayer's Greek Dictionary*:
1) dominion, power, lordship
2) in the NT: one who possesses dominion

Part of Speech: noun feminine
Total KJV Occurrences: 4

Translated as follows:
dominion, 2
Eph. 1:21; Jude 1:8
dominions, 1
Col. 1:16
government, 1
2 Pet. 2:10

Jude 1:8
KJV
> Likewise G3668 also G2532 these G3778 filthy
> dreamers G1797 defile G3392 the flesh G4561, despise
> G114**dominion** G2963, and speak G987 evil G987 of
> dignities G1391.

NKJV
> Likewise also these dreamers defile the flesh,
> reject **authority,** and speak evil of dignitaries.

NLT
> In the same way, these people—who claim
> authority from their dreams—live immoral lives,
> defy authority, and scoff at supernatural beings.

Chapter 10

My Plea

If you have thoughtfully read the Scriptures in Chapters 5 and 7, you now know, if you did not know before, that the Greek word *exousia*[G1849] defines the power and authority of both God's kingdom and Satan's kingdom.

To clarify, *exousia*[G1849] translates as power and authority. Of the 103 times *exousia* appears in the Bible, it refers to Satan's kingdom 19 times, that is about 20% of the time.

As of the writing of this book, I have been in the church for over 35 years. I have never heard it mentioned anywhere. I have read dozens of books by Christian authors about authority in the church, including: Watchman Nee, Bill Gothard, Kenneth Copeland, Kenneth Hagan, John Haggy, Billy Graham, Andy Stanly, Adrian Rodgers, Andrew Wommack, etc. Yet, none of them ever mentioned it.[9]

---

[9] If you are aware of anyone who has defined the difference, please contact me @ www.ourgodgivenrights.com.

What Did Jesus Say About Authority?

While all agree we are in a spiritual battle, no one ever explains that the same Greek word in the Bible that defines the power and authority of God's kingdom we are to submit to, also defines the power and authority of Satan's kingdom that we, as Christians, fight against.

Do our leaders in the church not know this fact? If not, why? How can they teach the Biblical truth about authority while omitting this vital fact? The Greek word *exousia,* which in scripture defines the authority of God's kingdom — is, used 20% of the time in Scripture to define the power of Satan's kingdom. The Scriptures that verify this are in chapter 7.

If our church leaders know this fact, why are they not teaching it? Are they afraid? What are they trying to hide something? Or, just ignoring this fact? If so, why?

Come on! I surely believe, at least I hope, our church leaders have more integrity then that. Therefore, I can only assume they do not know.

We need answers! There are authorities in the church who have engaged in the *exousia* Scripture ascribes to Satan's kingdom thinking. They exercise the *exousia* of God!

In my case, it nearly destroyed my life! When confronted, these authorities acted clueless and referred to the foundation of their ministry, Romans

What Did Jesus Say About Authority?

13:1–2, "all authority is of God, whoever resists authority resists what God established and receives condemnation." Thus, they threw out the foundation of Jesus' ministry appointed to the church, which is to give life, not condemn, as stated in John 3:16–17. Perhaps, these authorities were clueless as to the source of their *exousia*, as I have never found this Biblical fact outside of my studies of the Bible.

Jesus told Paul the following:

Acts 28:15–18 (NKJV)
So I said, 'Who are You, Lord?' And He said, 'I am Jesus, whom you are persecuting. But rise and stand on your feet; for I have appeared to you for this purpose, to make you a minister and a witness both of the things which you have seen and of the things which I will yet reveal to you. I will deliver you from the *Jewish* people, as well as *from* the Gentiles, to whom I now send you, to open their eyes, *in order* to turn *them* from darkness to light, and *from* the power (*exousia*) of Satan to God, that they may receive forgiveness of sins and an inheritance among those who are sanctified by faith in Me.'

How is it possible to deliver people from the power (*exousia*) of Satan if the church leadership does not know how to distinguish between the *exousia* that belongs to God's kingdom and the *exousia* that Scripture ascribes to Satan's kingdom?

Go ahead and be the first person to define the

difference between the *exousia* of these two kingdoms, as I have never heard or seen it done!

I implore you to do this. The lives and spiritual well-being of believers and many churches are at stake. If you are a leader in your church or home, you are responsible for leading believers to Christ and enabling them to stand in the power/authority (*exousia*) of God to overcome the power (*exousia*) of darkness. You can only do this if you truly understand and can define the difference between the *exousia* of these two kingdoms.

To make myself clear, the *exousia* of Satan has been defeated on the cross. Every believer has *exousia* as a gift from Jesus because of our belief in Him as the Son of God, our Savior, to overcome the *exousia* of darkness.

Awareness is the first step in walking in and exercising our God-given rights to our *exousia* over the *exousia* of darkness.

It is up to us to take personal responsibility to exercise this *exousia*. Failure to understand and exercise this *exousia* leaves us in defeat, even though Jesus defeated the *exousia* of Satan on the cross.

I offer how I came to understand the difference between the *exousia* of these two kingdoms.

First, how did humanity come under the *exousia* of

What Did Jesus Say About Authority?

By violating the first commandment and following the deceptive advice of Lucifer. Lucifer was a high-ranking angel, by all accounts, one of God's delegated authorities who strayed, exalted himself, pursued his selfish ambitions and was kicked out of Heaven, taking a third of the angels with him. He had a personal vendetta against God. He wanted to have *exousia* over the whole world. However, God had given this *exousia* to Adam. Thus, through deception, Satan stole this *exousia* from Adam, gaining *exousia* over the whole world and leading to our eternal damnation for joining Satan's rebellion.

But God so loved the world that He sent His only beloved Son, Jesus. On the cross, Jesus overcame the *exousia* of Satan by His obedience to God. He restored our God-given rights to the *exousia* God had given to Adam, giving us full rights as children of the living God..

Defining the difference between the *exousia* of these two kingdom has to do with what someone *does* with the *exousia* they have been given.

The first definition of *exousia* from *Thayer's Greek Dictionary* reads:

1. power of choice, liberty of doing as one pleases

This definition agrees with what Joshua said to the

people as they came into the Promised Land:

Joshua 24:14–15 (NKJV)
"Now therefore, fear the LORD, serve Him in sincerity and in truth, and put away the gods which your fathers served on the other side of the River and in Egypt. Serve the LORD! And if it seems evil to you to serve the LORD, choose for yourselves this day whom you will serve, whether the gods which your fathers served that *were* on the other side of the River, or the gods of the Amorites, in whose land you dwell. But as for me and my house, we will serve the LORD."

It is what someone chooses to do with the *exousia* God has given to them that matters. Do they choose to give life or condemn? Do they promote keeping and honoring the first commandment or violating it to follow and commit to teachings, traditions, and visions of men?

Do authorities really give freedom, not just conditionally offer it, to enslave people with manmade doctrines to build a ministry?

Do the authorities uphold and maintain the foundational purpose for ministry as appointed to the church by Jesus to give life, as stated in John 3:16 and Luke 4:18? Or have the authorities strayed from and/or rejected Jesus' foundation for ministry and now use Romans 13:1–2 as their foundation for ministry? Do they judge and condemn those who rightly honor the first commandment? Moreover, do they condemn those who wisely refuse to submit to having authority exercised over them and reject the "fear of judgment" introduced to motivate "works of ministry" to build a man's vision?

Such expression of authority Jesus defined as being of this world whose ruler is Satan. Furthermore, Jesus said it does not belong among His people. Using fear of judgment to motivate someone to do "works of ministry" does not express God's love and kindness. Fear has torment. It robs our peace. Perfect love casts out fear. God's love is perfect and it brings us peace. Believers are *not* to submit to a spirit of fear. For God has not given us a spirit of fear, but love, peace and a sound mind. So how could fear of judgment be part of God's equation in motivating "works of ministry" to share God's love and kindness to a lost and dying world?

Titus 3:4–7 (NLT)
> But—"When God our Savior revealed his kindness and love, he saved us, not because of the righteous things we had done, but because of his mercy. He washed away our sins, giving us a new birth and new life through the Holy Spirit. He generously poured out the Spirit upon us through Jesus Christ our Savior. Because of his grace he declared us righteous and gave us confidence that we will inherit eternal life."

Authentic "works of ministry" come from the heart because of a love for God and His people, to do what Jesus sent His church to do. Helping humanity receive their God-given rights to the fullness of their salvation bestowed upon them by Jesus.

If we refuse to hear and address these negative issues in the church, then we are exercising our *exousia* to reject the voice of God as spoken by all 12 Minor Prophets and the 5 Major Prophets in the Bible. These prophets said many negative things about authorities who were violating God's covenant and leading His people to violate God's covenant, which separated the nation from God and forfeited His blessing and protection. We could not hear the words of Jesus, as He said many negative things about religious authorities who were exercising their *exousia* in violation of God's law and God's appointed foundation and purpose for "works of ministry"—which kept people from God and His freedom and blessings.

Ezekiel summed up most of the negative things said by the prophets in the Old Testament:

Ezekiel 34:1–10 (NKJV)

> And the word of the LORD came to me,
> saying, "Son of man, prophesy against the
> shepherds of Israel, prophesy and say to them,
> 'Thus says the Lord GOD to the shepherds:
> "Woe to the shepherds of Israel who feed
> themselves! Should not the shepherds feed the
> flocks? You eat the fat and clothe yourselves
> with the wool; you slaughter the fatlings, *but* you
> do not feed the flock. The weak you have not

strengthened, nor have you healed those who were sick, nor bound up the broken, nor brought back what was driven away, nor sought what was lost; but with force and cruelty you have ruled them. So they were scattered because *there was* no shepherd; and they became food for all the beasts of the field when they were scattered. My sheep wandered through all the mountains, and on every high hill; yes, My flock was scattered over the whole face of the earth, and no one was seeking or searching *for them.*"

'Therefore, you shepherds, hear the word of the LORD: "*As* I live," says the Lord GOD, "surely because My flock became a prey, and My flock became food for every beast of the field, because *there was* no shepherd, nor did My shepherds search for My flock, but the shepherds fed themselves and did not feed My flock"— therefore, O shepherds, hear the word of the LORD! Thus says the Lord GOD: "Behold, I *am* against the shepherds, and I will require My flock at their hand; I will cause them to cease feeding the sheep, and the shepherds shall feed themselves no more; for I will deliver My flock from their mouths, that they may no longer be food for them."

I hope and pray Jesus Christ never says the same about anyone who reads this book, as the *exousia* expressed by the shepherds in this prophesy expose many things:

- They were not fulfilling the purpose of the

> "works of ministry" appointed by Jesus
- They were engaging in principles of authority of this world whose ruler is Satan, as defined by Jesus and forbidden by Him
- They did not uphold, follow, or hold fast to the qualifications for having or being in authority over God's people
- They were not taking care of the sheep
- They were rebelling against God's appointed purpose for authority
- They misused authority for personal gain
- They were self-serving instead of serving the people
- They did not care what happened to people
- They destroyed the flock
- They were unwilling to leave the 99 to find the lost sheep

Ezekiel's prophecy also clarifies that God will send someone to confront the shepherds who stray, as He cares for them and wants them to return to their first love.

Sadly, rather than returning to God, they destroyed or killed many of these messengers sent by God to call His people back to His ways.

If we truly want revival—not just pay lip service to that term to build a ministry or church—we must do what God said to Solomon after the House of the Lord was finished.

2 Chronicles 7:14–17 (NKJV)

What Did Jesus Say About Authority?

If My people who are called by My name will humble themselves, and pray and seek My face, and turn from their wicked ways, then I will hear from heaven, and will forgive their sin and heal their land. Now My eyes will be open and My ears attentive to prayer *made* in this place. For now I have chosen and sanctified this house, that My name may be there forever; and My eyes and My heart will be there perpetually. As for you, if you walk before Me as your father David walked, and do according to all that I have commanded you, and if you keep My statutes and My judgments.

I believe the difference between the *exousia* of God's kingdom, and Satan's kingdom concerns how and why *exousia* is used. In the hands of one person, *exousia* can bring death, while in the hands of another person it can bring life.

An example is found in the book of Esther. Haman was put in authority by the king who gave him a signet ring to symbolize that authority. Mordecai, a Jew and godly man, who *honored the first commandment*, refused to bow to Haman. Mordecai's defiance infuriated Haman, who exercised his *exousia* to condemn and destroy all of God's people. When Esther exposed the plot, Haman was hung on the gallows he built for Mordecai. The king gave Mordecai the same signet ring, symbolizing his *exousia*, which Mordecai used to deliver God's people.

What Did Jesus Say About Authority?

It all comes down to what is in the heart and the motives of a person who exercises *exousia*—the foundation for doing "works of ministry."

Is the foundation for doing "works of ministry" based on John 3:16–17, the foundation of Jesus' ministry? Jesus came to give life, not condemn. Giving life includes helping humanity receive their God-given rights to the fullness of their salvation bestowed upon every believer by Jesus. And, turning them from the *exousia* of Satan to God. Jesus appointed all authority in the church to bring us into the fullness of Christ (Eph. 4:13), this includes the fullness of our salvation from the *exousia* of Satan.

Is the foundation for "works of ministry" based on Romans 13:1–2, where people are judged and condemned if they refuse to submit to authorities exercising authority over them, and reject the fear of judgment threaten by authorities trying to enslave them to do "works of ministry" to build their organization? This is how the Bible says, the Beast—the ultimate manifestation of the spirit of the anti-christ—will build his kingdom. He will judge and condemn those who will not submit to his *exousia* and take his number, 666 (Rev. 13).

Here are a few verses that use the word *exousia* to verify it is why or how *exousia* is used that matters.

He taught as one having *exousia*, and not as the scribes (Matt. 7:29),

What Did Jesus Say About Authority?

Jesus said, "Whoever believes in Him has the *exousia* to become a child of God" (John 1:12).

Blessed are those who do His commands, that they may have the *exousia* to the tree of life, and may enter through the gates into the city. (Rev. 22:14.)

Beware lest somehow this *exousia* of yours becomes a stumbling block to those who are weak. (1 Cor. 8:9.)

Jesus sent out the twelve and gave them *exousia* over unclean spirits (Mark 6:7).

Jesus gave us *exousia* to tread on serpents and scorpions and over all the power of the enemy (Luke 10:19).

Saul had *exousia* from the leading priests to imprison and put to death the saints who believed in Jesus (Acts 26:10).

And they worshipped the dragon which gave *exousia* unto the beast and they worshipped the beast. (Rev. 13:4)

And there came out of the smoke locusts upon the earth, and unto them was given *exousia* as the scorpions of the earth have *exousia* (Rev. 9:3).

Paul emphasized his *exousia* was for edification and not destruction (2 Cor. 13:10).

What Did Jesus Say About Authority?

Pilate said to Jesus, "Do you not know I have the *exousia* to crucify you and the *exousia* to release you?" (John 19:10)

Ananias and Sapphira had *exousia* to decide what to do with the money from their property sale. Satan influenced their *exousia* as they lied about it to God and the church (Acts 5:4).

Having disarmed principalities and *exousia*, He made a public spectacle of them (Col. 2:15).

Jesus said to Paul, "I am sending you to open their eyes, and turn them from darkness to light, from the *exousia* of Satan to God" (Acts 26:18).

Now let us look at Peter.

Matthew 16:23 (NKJV)
But He turned and said to Peter, "Get behind Me, Satan! You are an offense to Me, for you are not mindful of the things of God, but the things of men."

Jesus had just told His disciples He was going to Jerusalem to be the sacrificial Lamb at the Passover. Peter tried to stop Jesus from going to the cross by exercising authority over Him. He told Jesus that he was not going to allow that to happen.

Peter had plans for Jesus that did not include watching his best friend, and presumptive future king of Israel, die slowly on the cross. Doing so would have ended everything Peter perceived to be in his future. Even though Peter was willing to fight to the death, he still did not understand the *exousia* of God's kingdom.

Satan was attempting to influence one of Jesus' three closes friends to stop Jesus from fulfilling His calling on His life.

Jesus was aware His battle was not against Peter, but that Satan had influenced the *exousia* exercised by Peter to upend the redemption and deliverance of humanity from the *exousia* of Satan's kingdom of darkness. Jesus rebuked him accordingly.

While Jesus has given everyone *exousia* in their lives as a gift to overcome the *exousia* of darkness, Jesus gives *exousia* as a church leader by qualification of character and motives of the heart as listed in Scripture to do the will of the Father. Building a ministry without those qualifications as the foundation and purpose for ministry—and accountability to maintain them—morphs it into a false ministry that will destroy many lives if left unchecked. The "works of ministry" performed by the elders and deacons of the Peoples Temple I mentioned in Chapter 2 are a good example.

Are you truly and confidently aware of whether the *exousia* in your life comes from Gods' kingdom or Satan's kingdom? The obvious answer is yes! How dare that even be questioned?

What Did Jesus Say About Authority?

However, if you cannot confidently explain the difference between the *exousia* Scripture ascribes to these two kingdoms, with full conviction, and teach it to your congregation so they too can understand, do you really know for sure? If you cannot answer this question, how can you be truthful before God, yourself, and the people you lead, as you stand before them and say, "I am God's delegated authority?"

www.ingramcontent.com/pod-product-compliance
Lightning Source LLC
Chambersburg PA
CBHW070613170726
48004CB00018B/1193